JANE ~
WHEN I Think of

Melissa and Sissy wisely and gently uncover some of the
most complicated years of our growing up. With unmatched
counseling experience, vulnerable story-telling and Biblical
foundation, this book shines a much needed light on the
intricacies of what it means to be a teenage girl today. While
perusing its pages I couldn't stop thinking - If only I had a book
like this during my teenage years! I would have devoured it.

Kelly Minter, Speaker, Author, Worship Leader

of How You have Always Greeted ME,

refuge always!

"I have my role models. They are truth-sharers and
truth-seekers. Sissy and Melissa have not only offered
me a revelational understanding of myself, but have
taught and challenged me to grow further in the ways
I was specifically designed to."

Katie, age 17

AT Church of AT School And that is
So WARMLY, so — You make me

"Melissa and Sissy have helped me so much. I wish I had
them on speed dial!"

Molly, age 17

Feel special + I have The sense
that is how you make many others
Feel, too. I will miss you in
middle school, but look forward
to seeing how God blesses + uses you
Throughout your HIGH School Days.
MUCH LOVE, Phil

youth specialties

Growing Up Without Getting Lost: Discovering Your Identity in Christ
Copyright 2008 by Melissa Trevathan and Sissy Goff

Youth Specialties products, 300 S. Pierce St., El Cajon, CA 92020 are published by Zondervan, 5300 Patterson Ave. SE, Grand Rapids, MI 49530.

ISBN 978-0-310-27917-4

Cover design by SharpSeven Design
Interior design by Brandi K. Etheredge

Printed in the United States of America

08 09 10 11 12 • 18 17 16 15 14 13 12 11 10 9 8 7 6 5 4 3 2 1

GROWING UP
without getting lost

By Melissa Trevathan and Sissy Goff

This book is dedicated to the Daystar summer interns
who have taught us so much during our writing years:
Celia, Briana, Lauren, Betsie, Clare, Jessica, Kathleen, Erin,
Caitlin, Chelsea, Aubrey, and Martha. You have been a constant
source of laughter, hope, encouragement and inspiration to us.
Satan can't live in our thankful hearts.

Anne Lamott says that her best prayers are "Help me, help me,
help me" and "Thank you, thank you, thank you." We have prayed
both of them often in the writing of these two books. And we have
spoken them (probably not often enough) to a group of people who
have helpedlighten our loads during our chaotic counseling/book
writing/summer camp directing kind of schedule. From a publishing
standpoint, we are grateful for the wisdom of Sandy VanderZicht,
Bob Hudson, Londa Alderink, Karen Campbell, Michael Ranville,
Kristie Fry, Jay Howver, Roni Meek, and Carla Barnhill. From a
don't-know-how-we-would-do-life-without-them standpoint, we
are grateful for the long-suffering of our families and friends.
And, of course, our dogs, Noel and Molasses.

Dear Fellow Travelers,

Life is strange and abstract. Life as a girl is perhaps even more strange and abstract. We are messy and determined, lovely and lonely, needy and stressed out.

The first time I met Sissy and Melissa I realized that my strange life as a girl meant something. It meant I was wired and designed to long for relationship and purpose. It also meant that, because life does not always provide perfect relationship or patent purpose, I was, as the old hymn goes, "prone to wander."

I have known these two women for six years now, and their encouragement and advice have changed my life. They have a rare combination of wisdom and humor, depth and simplicity, sincerity and straightforwardness. I am proud to call them my mentors, my role models, and my dearest friends—and I am proud to share them with you.

May we take the time to listen!

—Chelsea, 19

Table of Contents

An Introduction   7

Part One: Who Am I?
Chapter 1: You Are Here   13
Chapter 2: The Ruling Years (Birth to Ten): The Low Points   18
Chapter 3: The Ruling Years (Birth to Ten): The High Points   25
Chapter 4: The "It's All About Me" Years (11 to 14):
        The Low Points   31
Chapter 5: The "It's All About Me" Years (11 to 14):
        The High Points   38
Chapter 6: The "Are We There Yet?" Years (15 and 16):
        The Low Points   48
Chapter 7: The "Are We There Yet?" Years (15 and 16):
        The High Points   56
Chapter 8: The Independent—More or Less—Years (17 to 19):
        The Low Points   62
Chapter 9: The Independent —More or Less—Years (17 to 19):
        The High Points   73

Part Two: What Do I Want In Life?
Chapter 10: With the Heart   79
Chapter 11: Relentless Reminders   85
Chapter 12: The Relationship Chapter: Girls   93
Chapter 13: The Relationship Chapter: Guys   102
Chapter 14: Returning Thanks   107
Chapter 15: Giving Grace   114

Part Three: What Should I Do?
Chapter 16: Harmless Habits   125
Chapter 17: Hard Habits to Break   137
Chapter 18: Words of Wisdom   152

Part Four: Who Do I Want to Be?
Chapter 19: The Action of Mercy   159
Chapter 20: You Matter   166

Epilogue – Lost... and Found   171
Notes   174

An Introduction

I (Sissy) am terrified of ventriloquist dummies. I'm pretty sure it has something to do with the first time I got really lost.

When I was eight, my mom took my cousin Blair and me to see a double feature at the drive-in theater. After sitting in the car for several hours, Blair and I started to feel a little cramped. We decided to stretch our legs by heading over to the concession stand for drinks and popcorn.

We climbed out of my mom's car and started wandering through the maze of vehicles. We walked for what seemed like a long time before we finally saw the concessions stand. Blair and I loaded up on all of the drinks, popcorn, and candy we could carry. We turned around to head back to the car, and had no idea where to find my mom.

Even though we had walked for a long time to get to the concession stand, I expected to see my mom's blue Volvo in the first row. Instead there was a sea of cars, all of them looking blue in the darkness. Nervously, Blair and I started walking in what we hoped was the right direction, peering through car windows and calling "Mom" every few steps.

It felt like the night was getting darker and darker, as we walked. We couldn't find my mom anywhere. I was beyond worried—I was panicked. And then I heard it. A hideous, monstrous laugh poured out of the speakers sitting in the windows of the cars around us (back in the "good old days" of drive-ins, we had to hang a speaker in the car window in order to hear the movie). I looked up at the screen and saw the huge, crazy, scary face of a ventriloquist dummy. In the plot of the movie this dummy had come to life and was taking over the mind of his ventriloquist. His maniacal cackle nearly scared me to death.

I have never forgotten how it felt to be lost that night. I have never forgotten that sense of terror that cut through me when I heard that laughter. And I have never forgotten how certain I was that I would never find my way back to safety.

Nearly everyone we know has a story about being lost. You probably have one, too. Maybe you were in a crowd and reached for your sister's hand, only to find you were holding on to someone you didn't know. Maybe you absentmindedly got into a car after practice one afternoon and turned to see someone else's dad in the driver's seat. Maybe you got separated from your mom in the grocery store. Or maybe you got lost and ended up in a strange neighborhood the first time you drove home by yourself.

No matter how we get lost, the feelings that come along with the lostness are the same—panic, confusion, frustration. It feels like every turn, every step, is wrong. It feels like you will never make it home.

Getting lost

It's easy for girls to get lost in these growing-up years. We're not talking about lost in location, like in the department store or amusement park, although that obviously happens, too. We're talking about a deeper kind of lost. This kind of lost has more to do with *who* you are than *where* you are.

When you were a little girl life was pretty simple. You knew

who you were—in a very elementary-school sort of way. Good was good. Bad was bad. The people you loved were close to perfect. Life went along without too many bumps.

But then things changed. Life didn't make sense in quite the same way. Good and bad—well, they got kind of mixed up. The people you loved started to disappoint you. *You* disappointed you. You had feelings and thoughts that surprised you—and not in a good way. You did things that surprised everyone around you—also not in a good way. This is all part of getting lost.

How do we know, you might wonder? How do we know what it feels like to be lost like that—especially if we're old enough to remember drive-in movies? (And Melissa has much clearer memories of them than I do, if you know what I mean.)

We know because we talk to lost girls every day. We are both counselors at a place called Daystar Counseling Ministries in Nashville, Tennessee. We have the honor of sitting with girls, much like you, who are struggling. They are lost, wandering from place to place—and sometimes from identity to identity—trying to figure out who they are.

I (Melissa) remember meeting with a girl who dressed in all black and wore heavy dark makeup. Her parents were worried about the way she dressed. They thought it might be a sign that she was deeply troubled—maybe even depressed—and they wanted me to talk with her to find out what was going on.

Just a few weeks after we started meeting, this same girl bounded into my office wearing a yellow, smiley-face T-shirt and lots of brightly colored jewelry. When I looked at her with obvious surprise, she said, "Oh, I got tired of the whole Goth thing. I decided to be a skater instead." This girl was lost. She was trying on identities like they were pairs of sunglasses.

Even if you haven't changed your image in such a drastic way, it's likely you still feel a little lost. You still know the panic of wandering around, not really knowing which way to go.

In these years between 15 and 19, you are bombarded with pressure. You're supposed to get good grades without getting too stressed out. You're supposed to earn your parents' trust and your friends' respect; live up to your potential but not stress about being perfect; look toward the future but enjoy the present; exercise and eat right but not focus on your body image. You're supposed to fit in, stand out, be true to yourself, and impress other people. How could you not feel lost in the middle of all of that?

Asking questions

The girls we talk to are lost for many of the same reasons you are. They come to counseling because their parents are getting divorced, or they are struggling with friends, or they have gotten in trouble, or they have an eating disorder, or they're struggling with any one of the issues facing you or your friends on any given day. Basically they are wandering around in the circles of pressure and expectations, stress and school, friends and family. And in the midst of all of it, they are asking questions —questions we know you're asking, too.

Who am I?
What do I want in life?
What should I do?
Who do I want to be?

Our friend Anne turned 16 recently. She loved driving and would offer to go just about anywhere for her mom. She made up errands just so she could take the car. But there was one problem: Anne had a horrible sense of direction. It was always the same. About ten minutes after Anne would leave the house, her mom would get a phone call. Sure enough, it would be Anne, panicky, frustrated, and lost. "Mom, I need your help. Which way do I go?" Anne wasn't dumb. She wasn't trying to get lost. She just needed a guide—her mom on the other end of the phone—to help her find her way.

That's what we try to be to the girls we counsel—guides. We are helping them find their way through all the confusion of their teenage years. And that's what we want this book to do for you. We don't want to tell you which way to go—that would be *our* way out, not *yours*. Instead, we want to give you the tools you need to find your own way, a way that is unique to who you are and who God made you to be.

This book will be a journey we'll take together. We'll start with where you've been, then talk about where you are now. We'll look at what you want, and why certain things and people have the power to make you really happy—or really hurt. We'll talk about friends and families and boys, and how you can connect with these important people without losing yourself. We'll look at why you sometimes feel bad about yourself—and what will make you feel better. We'll walk through some of the harder issues such as alcohol and drugs, eating disorders, sex, and self-harm. And in the midst of all of these conversations, we think you'll begin to find your way.

God has made you unlike anyone else. He has given you strengths and talents and qualities and characteristics that will make a difference to the world. You won't fully understand all of that by the time you finish this book—you will spend a lifetime figuring out who God has made you to be. But our desire is that this book will help you start finding your way out of the confusion—finding yourself. Most of all, we hope this book will help you start feeling a little less lost.

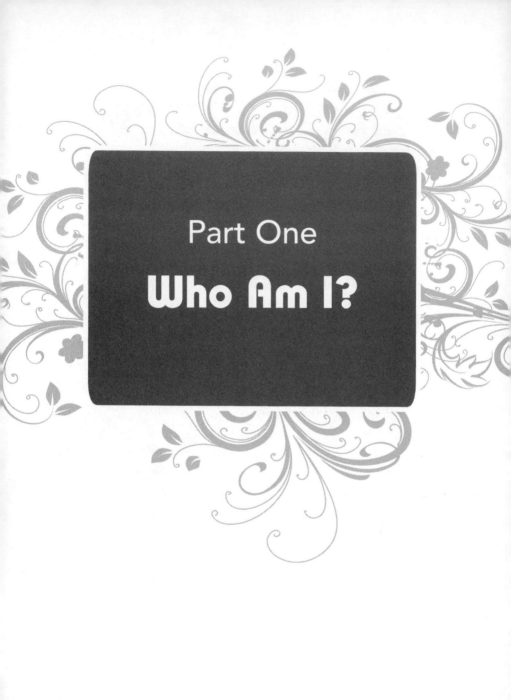

Part One

Who Am I?

Chapter 1
You Are Here

You must walk. It is a long journey, through a country that is sometimes pleasant and sometimes dark and terrible.
— *L. Frank Baum,* The Wizard of Oz

You've probably seen the movie *The Wizard of Oz* a number of times. Maybe you've even read the books about Dorothy and her adventures in the strange Land of Oz. But you've probably never thought about the similarities between the Land of Oz and junior high. Think about the scene where Dorothy lands in Munchkinland, walks out her door, and finds herself in a world of color. She discovers new, exciting things like munchkins and talking scarecrows and yellow brick roads. And she finds scary things like witches with green faces, flying monkeys, and a terrifying wizard. It's a world that's completely different from the one she knew back in Kansas.

Your early teenage years were probably a lot like Dorothy's experience in Oz. But this time the munchkins were the boys you couldn't quite figure out and the flying monkeys were the mean girls who came out of nowhere to rip into your self-esteem. It probably doesn't take much effort for you to remember how those years felt—confusing, scary, uncertain.

But now that you're a bit older things are different. You've kind of settled in to your Technicolor life. You have matured enough to know that mean girls can't destroy you with their insults and boys are less mysterious than you thought.

A few years ago a Broadway musical opened that told a slightly different version of the familiar tale of Oz. *Wicked* is the story behind the story. It's about the reasons why Glinda, the good witch, became "good" and Elphaba, the bad witch, became "bad." We first meet Glinda (known as Galinda in the first act of the play) and Elphaba when they are about to begin the Oz equivalent of college. Over the course of the play both of them go through all kinds of changes, the kind most girls experience in their teenage years. Elphaba starts out insecure. She tries to hide behind ugly dresses and weird glasses. She struggles to make friends and would rather be with animals than people. Glinda is insecure, too. But she covers her insecurity by acting like it's not there. Glinda's main goals in life are to be popular, attract the perfect boy, and intimidate other girls. Sound like anyone you knew in junior high?

By the end of the musical, though, both girls are different (but we won't give it away). They want more than popularity and attention, they want purpose. They want to connect with the people they love and know that they can make a difference in their world. They are true to themselves, even at significant cost. They have grown up.

Your journey is similar. When you were a child, you had a natural confidence in who you were. As you got older you lost it. Without it you didn't know what else to do but hide behind any number of cover-ups—being mean to your siblings, talking back to your parents, hanging out with kids who you knew might get you into trouble. But now you're on the road to finding your confidence again.

That part of the journey might be over, but we don't want you to forget it. As we talk about what the second half of your teenage years will look like, we want you to remember how

much you've already lived through. You have faced dark and terrible things—with friends, with your family, or inside of yourself. And you've had pleasant times—more than pleasant. You have had joy and hope and goodness in your life, even if you haven't always been able to recognize it. All of those parts of your story so far have combined to make you who you are and who you are becoming.

If you've had a psychology class in school, you've probably studied human development. If you haven't had a class like that, then maybe it sounds boring and clinical. But it's not. It's fascinating, mostly because it's like getting an inside peek at why people are the way they are. Human development explains why you wanted to hold and sing to your dolls while your brother wanted to blow them up. It explains why you used to think nothing of putting on a tutu and twirling around in front of your parents and their friends, but can't imagine doing anything like that now. It explains why other people have so much power over how you feel about yourself.

The truly amazing thing about development is that it never stops. You are constantly changing and growing in ways you can't predict. What was once a strength might be more of a struggle now and vice versa. Who you were three years ago is not necessarily who you are today. And who you are right now is not necessarily who you will be in three years. But along the way, God has been doing very specific things inside of you to help you become the woman you will be one day. No book could ever cover all these fascinating changes, so we'll just hit the high points—and some low points, too. But in the midst of all of these points, we want to remind you that development is all about—well —developing. It's about growing, and growing takes place in different ways and at different speeds for everyone.

Have you noticed that you've always had a few friends who looked (and maybe acted) several years younger or several years older than you? You might have started your period way earlier than your friends—or much later. There is no right or wrong speed for development. And there's definitely no hurry. It takes time to change from a child to an adult, and that's exactly what's happening to you right now.

So don't worry if you're the last of your friends to date or wear makeup, or even if you're the last of your friends to care about any of that. God made you to be uniquely you. That means you will develop in your own way and at your own speed. If it's taking you longer to develop, you will catch up. If you're developing quickly, you will just be a little ahead of your friends from time to time. Eventually every girl will go through the changes that come with being a teenager. You can't change the pace at which you're growing up, but you can enjoy the high points and learn how to hang in there during the low points. God is using them both to form you into the person you were created to be.

Getting there isn't always easy and every girl can use a little help along the way. We both love to snow ski. It's awesome—and sometimes totally confusing. A mountain is a very easy place to get lost. Thankfully, the people who develop ski areas know how quickly skiers can lose their way. So they have a great way of helping us out. As soon as you get off a ski lift at the top of a run there's a huge map of the entire mountain. The map itself is good, but the most helpful part is a little red dot with the words "You are here" written above it. Because if you don't know where you are, you have no idea where to go next. You end up stuck on the mountain.

The same is true for the journey to adulthood. The next few chapters on development will be your "You are here" sign. They will help you understand all that God has done inside of you so far. The better you understand how you got to this point, the better equipped you'll be for what's coming. After all, this is a journey of discovery, of knowing who you've been, who you are, and who you want to become.

Chapter 2
The Ruling Years
(Birth to Ten)

The Low Points

*I've had the same goal I've had ever since I was a girl.
I want to rule the world. — Madonna*

I (Melissa) wanted to rule the world when I was younger, too—or at least the merry-go-round on my playground at AB Austin Elementary School. Actually everyone at my school wanted to rule the merry-go-round. The goal was to become Queen—or King—of the merry-go-round. You earned this title by making your way from the outside edge of the merry-go-round to the stationary center, throwing off all rivals as you moved. Then with all the other boys and girls spinning sadly around you, you would stand triumphant.

I had a secret strategy for my takeover. I hung back, never participating in the merry-go-round wars, just watching and waiting for my time to come. Then one morning I knew I was ready. Wearing a dress my grandmother and aunt had made, I gracefully stomped across the playground, climbed onto the merry-go-round, held on for dear life, and pulled myself past the other kids.

And then it happened. I reached the center. I had conquered the merry-go-round! I was living out my grandest dream. The other kids whirled around me while I stood smiling—amazed and proud of myself. Until something went wrong. I stopped smiling because it became really hard to breathe. I looked down to see my dress winding tighter and tighter around my body. It had gotten caught in the gears! The kids kept spinning, and I started to get sick. My short experience as Queen ended with me throwing up and having to be cut out of my dress.

How do you think I felt walking back into school? Embarrassed? Humiliated? No, I felt like the ruler of the world.

In the first ten years of life, girls are free. We call these the Discovery Years (birth to five) and the Adventurous Years (six to eleven). During the first ten years you learned to walk, talk, run, jump, play sports, and ride your bike. You developed all kinds of other skills that made you feel confident—even though you were too young to know what confidence was. You were focused on having fun, not on what other people thought about you. You were learning and growing and conquering the world. You had high points and low points, but you handled both with that same freedom and confidence.

Although you were free and adventurous in those first ten years, there were certain areas of your life that were difficult, too. You may remember being scared of the monsters under your bed or feeling jealous of the attention your parents and everyone else gave your new little brother. These are some of the hard parts about being little—being a little girl, in particular.

These very same issues can continue to affect you today. That's why we want to talk about them.

Watch me!

What it meant then: Do you remember how important it was for your mom or dad to see you jump off the high dive or slide down the slide? In those first few years of life you said, "Watch me!" a lot. And if you've spent any time around young girls lately, you've probably heard it, too. Little girls are always shouting to their parents—or anyone else they want to impress—to drop everything and watch.

Little girls love to be noticed. They love to be applauded and appreciated. Basically they want attention. We say that girls want to be *delighted* in. They want the people they love to admire and enjoy them for who they are and what they can do. You still do. We still do. But the "watch me" call of your little girl years can become pretty obnoxious—even manipulative—as you get older.

What it means now: You may not be dramatic about it, shouting out for people to notice you, but you still want attention. You've just learned to be a little more subtle in your attempts to get it.

A friend of ours named Carrie spent her summers at camp. She had lots of good friends and they often had long, honest conversations about their lives. But sometimes, even in the middle of all those friends, Carrie would get lonely. When she did, she would wander out onto the dock at the lake. That would have been fine if she were out there because she wanted some time alone. But she wasn't. By walking out onto the dock, Carrie was shouting, "Watch me!" to the other kids at camp in a very quiet and very manipulative way. Carrie wanted attention. She wanted her friends to notice something was wrong and to follow her onto the dock to find out what it was.

What Carrie wanted was perfectly normal—we all want someone to notice when we're feeling hurt or upset. We want them to care enough to stop and check on us. But when we pull away just to see if someone will come after us, that's manipulative. And girls, we are great manipulators.

Instead of making your friends guess what you're feeling or testing them with little tricks to get their attention, trust them enough to tell them when something is wrong. They might not necessarily respond exactly the way you'd like (we'll talk more about that later). But wouldn't you rather have someone be concerned about you because they want to be, not because they've been manipulated into it?

If you want attention—if you want to be noticed and delighted in—be yourself. You don't have to have the perfect clothes or get the perfect grades or score the winning goal. You don't have to get in trouble or dress in ultra-revealing or even oddly mismatched clothes. All you have to do is be yourself. The kind of friends you really want will notice and love you more for being you, anyway.

You are delightful. No matter who you are or what you can or can't do—you are worthy of attention. God made you that way. And he is the one who delights in you most. Take a look at this verse from the book of Psalms: "He brought me out into a spacious place; he rescued me because he delighted in me" (Psalm 18:19).

Fears

What it meant then: Children have intense imaginations (some of us still do!), and that can make them afraid of made-up worlds filled with monsters and witches. Children can also be afraid of the real world; worrying that something bad might happen to them or someone they love. I (Sissy) wasn't just afraid of ventriloquist dummies. I was afraid of just about everything. My imagination had me terrified of falling off my bike, of one of my parents being hurt, and of the witch I was convinced lived in my closet.

We probably don't need to say much more about the fears of little girls; if you struggled with them you know all about them. But what you might not know is how those fears can stay with you—even paralyze you—for many years to come.

What it means now: Your imagination once had the power to totally freak you out. But hopefully there were grown-ups in your life who helped you understand that there were no monsters under your bed, no witches in the closet, no child-eating creatures scratching at your bedroom window. "You are safe," they would say. "Nothing bad is going to happen to you."

As you got older, you started to understand some of the realities of life—and that reality can be pretty scary, too. Houses really do get broken into. People are killed. Parents get divorced. Bad things happen every day. Your imagination still runs wild but now it's not those fantasy fears that worry you, it's the real stuff. It can be a lot harder for someone to convince you that you're safe when you know that's not always true.

That's where the paralysis comes in. Sometimes girls your age get so worried about something terrible happening that they stop enjoying life. They get stuck in their fears. For some girls, those fears involve people dying or being hurt—so they don't allow themselves to build close connections with people. For other girls, the fear of failure or embarrassment is enough to keep them from pursuing their dreams.

Our friend Elizabeth told us this story about fear. It's one we wanted you to hear, too:

The monster that lived in the closet of every other elementary school kid in America never visited my closet when I was little. Maybe the fact that my daddy was right down the hall kept him away, or maybe fear just didn't faze me as a child. I had read all the Nancy Drew mystery books by the end of third grade, and in fifth grade I was reading murder and kidnapping detective stories on a weekly basis. I just didn't scare easily.

All of that changed when I entered high school. All of a sudden the monster that was never in the closet transformed into some very real fears that kept me awake late into the night, clutching a key chain with a Bible verse and singing "Amazing Grace" under my breath while I listened and analyzed every single creak of the house. What I was scared of I couldn't tell you. Maybe I had heard too many horror stories on the news, or maybe those mystery books from my childhood were finally getting to me, but whatever was causing this sudden onset of fear was slowly beginning to take over my life.

I knew that monsters and ghosts weren't real, but I still wouldn't go to sleep without checking in my closet and underneath my bed. Logic told me that if I checked every nook and cranny when I walked into the room, nobody could appear ten minutes later. Logic, however, has little, if any, chance of convincing you when it's up against a monster as powerful as fear.

Now I'm a senior in high school and proud to say that I have, for the most part, conquered my fears. It took several long conversations with God before I was able to convince myself that my fears were unfounded and several more before I was willing to turn out my closet light without first checking to make sure it was empty. Slowly but surely, I handed my fears over to the Lord and trusted that he would take care of both them and me.

I know now that fear was just a tool Satan used to slowly build a brick wall between God and me. But with God's promise to never leave me or forsake me running through my mind, I slowly began tearing down that brick wall.

Sometimes at night I still jump on and off my bed so nothing can grab me. Even if the boogeyman still makes the occasional visit to my closet, the important thing is that I know God has complete control of my life. Like that old VeggieTales song says, "God is MUCH bigger than the boogeyman."

Fear can only be fought with faith. It was Elizabeth's faith that helped her learn God can take away fear. God will help you get rid of your fears, too—he helped me (Sissy) get rid of mine. But it took a long time and a lot of prayer. I have spent many nights sitting in my bed singing and praying and reading Scripture out loud—even as an adult. And I definitely still have to stay away from scary movies and books.

Bad things do happen, but God is present even in the midst of those bad things. You can trust that no matter what happens in your life, God will be with you, giving you the strength to handle it. There is nothing to fear when we have God at our side.

There are some beautiful Bible verses that remind us of how much God cares for us and that he is close to us even when we're afraid. Psalm 17:8 is a prayer that says, "Keep me as the apple of your eye; hide me in the shadow of your wings." In Psalm 23:4 David said, "Even though I walk through the darkest valley, I will fear no evil, for you are with me; your rod and your staff, they comfort me." And Psalm 28:6-7 reads, "Praise be to the Lord, for he has heard my cry for mercy. The Lord is my strength and my shield; my heart trusts in him, and he helps me. My heart leaps for joy, and with my song I praise him."

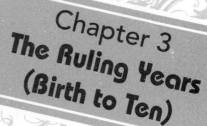

The High Points

Meg, wearing mackintosh boots and a red mackintosh, and with red sou'wester tied beneath her chin, splashed down the drive, and under the dripping oak trees, in a state of happiness deeper and more perfect than any other she was likely to know while she lived in this world. Had she known that she would never be happy in quite this way again she would not have been so happy, but she did not know. She was four years old, and much beloved, and regarded happiness as the normal state of everybody.

Elizabeth Goudge, The Heart of the Family

The high points of what God was doing in your first ten years definitely outweighed the low points—they always do. God was working on your brain, your heart, and your spirit. And you still carry all that work with you today.

Your brilliant brain

What it meant then: Mary Holland is two years old. She has three brothers who get in trouble from time to time. Brown, Will, or Ian might accidentally hit someone over the head with a toy, run when they're not supposed to, or commit some other kid-sized offense and be sent to time-out. Time-out is a really hard thing for Mary Holland—especially when her brothers are in it. Mary Holland's mom will look away for a minute, and Mary Holland will bring Will her favorite stuffed animal. Or she'll climb up on the counter to get a cookie for Brown. Or try to make Ian laugh.

At two years old, Mary Holland has something called oxytocin shooting through her brain. Oxytocin is a hormone that God has specifically placed inside the brains of girls. Boys have it too, but not in such a huge amount. Oxytocin is what causes Mary Holland to care. She has a built-in need to nurture and to love. You do, too. It's part of what God was developing in you even before you were born, and it's an important part of who you are today.

Other developments were going on in your brain back then, too. God was building very specific skills and strengths in you. And they were very different from those of boys. Here are some of the differences.

What You Could Do Compared to Boys	Inside Your Brain	What That Meant Then	What That Means Now
Speak earlier	The left hemisphere controls speech. It grows more quickly in girls than in boys.	This one is kind of easy; you could talk earlier than most boys.	When you're with your guy friends, you do most of the talking.
Control your emotions and responses	The female brain creates more serotonin, which has to do with impulse control, than the male brain. The limbic system, which manages emotions, also develops faster in girls than in boys.	When you were in preschool and elementary school, the boys got in more trouble than the girls.	When boys get angry, they tend to explode with strong words or actions. You probably simmer a little more—which can be good and bad.

What You Could Do Compared to Boys	Inside Your Brain	What That Meant Then	What That Means Now
Recognize different sights, smells, sounds, and feelings	The occipital lobe of the brain develops earlier in girls. That's the part that takes in information and feelings.	You could tell, even at a young age, when one of your parents was upset.	You understand the subtext of what your friends are saying—and what they're not saying. It's called "intuition."
Remember more and in greater detail	The hippocampus, which controls memory, is larger in girls' brains at this age.	You could tell your parents every little detail about your day—what the teacher wore, who sat where, and how you felt about it all.	You remember every detail of a date, an argument, or even a conversation.

What it means now: God designed girls to be connected with other people. He gave you gifts that help you love others and connect with them—even in the way he grew your brain in those first ten years.

Confidence

What it meant then: Confidence is a funny thing. Some days you have lots of it. Other days, not so much. And we would guess it was in particularly short supply in seventh and eighth grades. When you were younger, however, you had loads of it.

There are so many great stories I could tell you about when Melissa was a little girl (this is Sissy talking—and Melissa would hate that I'm saying this). She would do—and did do—just about anything.

She picked the flowers from her neighbors' yards without permission, thinking she was making a beautiful gift for her mom. She threw books off the balcony in church that "accidentally" hit people on the head. She decided it would be really fun to make an extra-long bicycle. So she had all of the kids in her neighborhood take off their front wheels to try to hook them together. Obviously it didn't work. Even more obviously, Melissa was a little bit of a troublemaker.

But she was confident. She didn't worry about what other people thought of her. And neither did you when you were younger. You might have been shyer than Melissa—I sure was. I don't mean the kind of shy that has to do with whether people are talking behind your back. I mean the kind of shy that comes from being a little unsure of other people, the kind that's not about you but about them.

When you were little you probably had moments of uncertainty. But for the most part, you spent your days discovering new skills and trying new activities. You learned to talk and walk and kick a ball and draw and ride a bike and play hopscotch. You didn't worry about scoring a goal or drawing well. You just did it. Every time you learned something new, your confidence grew a little more. And the more confident you became, the more you were willing to try.

You probably made friends in much the same way. You didn't rehearse how you were going to ask a friend to play with you at recess. You just asked. But if you're like most girls your age, you practice all kinds of conversations in your room now—telling your friend that she hurt your feelings, asking a boy to the Sadie Hawkins dance, begging your parents for a cell phone. You rehearse because you want it to go well, and you're not sure it will.

What it means now: You were naturally confident during

those first ten years. Somewhere in junior high you lost it—or at least a lot of it. We want you to regain some of the confidence from those early years. Better yet, we want to help you develop a more mature kind of confidence. We want you to feel good about who you are and who God is helping you to be. Even if you're not a Mia Hamm or Mary Cassatt in the making, you still have a lot to offer the world. Throughout this book our desire is to help you figure out just what that is.

Awareness

What it meant then: I (Sissy) have a blind dog. She is a 15-year-old Maltese named Noël and she is tiny. Because she's so little, I've always worried about her. But my worries got worse when she started going blind.

It happened right before we were heading to camp for the summer. Here at Daystar, summer brings a whole new schedule. We bring the kids up to Kentucky for a camp called "Camp Hopetown." We have six different camps built around various age groups. The camp I was most worried about was the one for those in second, third, and fourth grades. Those of us on staff call it our "sprint camp." We never sit down because they never really sit down. The five days with those kids at camp are the wildest, busiest, most chaotic days of our summer. They are also some of our most fun. But not for Noël.

Even before she lost her sight, Noël didn't really like second-through-fourth-grade camp. Everyone wanted to pick her up. They wanted to love her and squeeze her, and they completely overwhelmed her (without meaning to, of course). I couldn't even imagine what that week of camp would be like for Noël now that she was blind.

When the kids first arrived at camp that year, I talked to

them about blind dogs—that they had to speak to Noël before they touched her so she would know they were coming, for example. And you know what? Out of all six of our camps, the elementary kids were the sweetest to Noël. They would start talking to her from several feet away. They were gentle and patient. One of them even made her a walking stick with her name painted on the side. This is the kind of awareness girls have in their first ten years.

You may not remember being aware, but you were. Ask the adults in your life. They probably have stories of your kindness to animals or your tenderness with older people and babies. We have heard so many stories of girls in elementary school who were kind to handicapped kids or who wrote notes to friends who were sad.

What it means now: Unlike confidence, awareness doesn't fade as you get older. Instead it shifts. Junior high girls are consumed with themselves and what other people think of them. In high school, though, things shift again. Your focus is more on how you can care about others than on what they think of you. You're settling in with a group of friends who accept you for who you are. And you've started to realize that the people who don't accept you probably won't be the kind of friends you want anyway.

God has given you so many strengths that started way back in your first ten years. Those parts of your childhood that sometimes made life hard don't have to define who you are. And all the great aspects of being a confident, aware little girl are still inside you, ready to be part of the amazing person you are becoming.

Chapter 4
The "It's All About Me" Years (11-14)

The Low Points

Cherylanne is fourteen, and she is pretty. I am twelve and I am not, although Cherylanne said this is the awkward stage and I could just as likely get better. We watch.

— *Elizabeth Berg,* Durable Goods

Our friend Monique says the very best part of being in high school is that you no longer believe the world revolves around you. But between the ages of 11 and 14, most girls are convinced it does.

Several years ago at camp we talked about development with a group of seventh and eighth graders. We used a word many parenting experts use to describe girls in this age group: *Narcissistic.*

We explained how narcissism is basically selfishness taken to the next level. It is an intense preoccupation with yourself, what other people think about you, what you think about you, and anything else that has to do with you. One of the girls in the back of the room raised her hand.

"I am so excited to know about this word. My parents call me selfish a lot. But I secretly have always known that selfish wasn't quite enough. It's narcissistic—I am narcissistic!" And she didn't even laugh.

The years from 11 to 14 are very complicated and very serious. Many of the teenage girls we know would say these were the hardest years of growing up so far. You might feel the same way. Mean girls, insecurities, sarcastic boys, pressure, and chaotic hormones all jumble together to make for some tough days. But even in those difficult years God is at work, using all of those low points to form you into you.

Ambivalence

What it meant then: I (Sissy) met with a girl recently—a girl very much in her "it's-all-about-me" years—who told me that her main goal in life was to annoy her parents. And then, in the very next breath, she told me how badly she wanted them to love her. This is ambivalence in its truest form. It is saying "come close" and "get away" at the same time.

Every young teenager feels some degree of ambivalence—most of it directed at her parents. You felt it when you wanted your mom to come in and rub your back when you were falling asleep, then once she got there you got irritated by everything she said. Come close…get away. It's why you wanted your dad to help you with your homework but grunted and told him you could do it on your own once he offered his assistance. Come close…get away.

All of that ambivalence had to do with your growing sense of independence. You were moving from a little girl to a teenager. You wanted to be your own person but still have someone take care of you. You had one foot in each world and you kept shifting from one to the other. You knew your parents weren't going anywhere, so they were an easy outlet for whatever frustration you might have been feeling.

Independence is complicated for everyone involved, even your parents. It's not just that you were hard to figure out in those years. It's that your parents have their own sense of ambivalence as you've moved through your teen years. They want you to grow up, but they also want to hold on to you.

Strange as it might sound, that ambivalence helped you gain confidence. It helped you wander out into the world because you knew you could come back to the safety of the people who love you. You're still doing the same thing and will—to some degree—forever. We all want to take risks, but we want to take them within a safe, supportive environment. And because your parents were your first safe, supportive environment, they sometimes got the brunt of your wandering— especially during the narcissistic phase of your life.

What it means now: Your wandering looks different now that you're older. You can ask people to come close as you build healthy relationships. You are learning to say something that sounds and feels a little better than "get away." You can talk to your parents and gently help them understand your need to take your own risks, discover your own ideas, and make your own decisions. You can be close to them without feeling like it will stifle your independence. Ambivalence not only helps you gain confidence, it also helps you find the crucial balance between connection and space, closeness and independence, that will be a part of all your relationships to come.

Self-consciousness

What it meant then: Do you remember when you first thought someone was watching you? Not watching in a weird way but in a critical way. Maybe it was when you wanted your dad to stop kissing you good-bye when you got out of the car at school because you knew the older girls were watching. Or maybe it happened when you didn't want your brothers and sisters to goof around in public because you felt like other people were staring at your family. Maybe it was the first time you realized that what you were wearing wasn't really like what everyone else was wearing, and you felt a little awkward.

Psychologists talk about something called an imaginary audience. It means between the ages of 11 and 14 you believed—-very strongly—there were people watching everything you did and listening to everything you said. This caused you immense amounts of embarrassment any time you or your family did anything you thought was out of the ordinary. The reality, which you know now, is there was no audience—which, obviously, is the imaginary part. The people you thought were watching were really only thinking about the people they thought were watching them.

All of this watching and not watching is one of the big reasons girls are plagued by self-consciousness in these years. They live in an almost perpetual state of embarrassment. From an emotional standpoint, it's unbearable. From a physical standpoint, it's surprisingly explainable.

Have you ever turned on your hair dryer while your straightener was warming up and your computer was running and your iPod speakers were blaring? Then you know what happens. Suddenly everything shuts off—you've blown a fuse. When there's too much electricity running through the wires the circuit shorts out and the power shuts off, until someone resets it. The same thing happened in your brain when you hit puberty.

When you were a baby, your brain grew really fast. You were developing new connections and neural pathways, your hormones were firing up, you were learning at an amazing pace. When you were a little girl, that growth slowed down. You were obviously still learning, but not nearly as much or as quickly as before. Then your hormones started rumbling again and your brain clicked into high gear once more. Your brain began to change like crazy, with new connections and pathways. And sometimes all that activity made your brain short-circuit. But rather than going out entirely—like electricity—it caused something we call a hiccup in confidence.

You can probably guess what those hiccups looked like. You woke up one morning and felt like all your friends were mad at you when they really weren't. You got home after school and dissolved into tears for no reason. You wanted to try out for the school musical but didn't dare because you thought someone might laugh at you.

Self-consciousness is one of the biggest struggles for 11- to-14-year-old girls. They are so afraid of standing out in a negative way that they often stop standing out entirely. They forget—or ignore—the wonderful people God has made them to be because they are so focused on what others might think of them.

What it means now: As girls grow older, that self-consciousness can sometimes turn into self-hatred, which is when you stop worrying that other people don't like you and you decide you don't like yourself. We'll talk more about that later in the book. For now, we want you to know if you're feeling some of that self-hatred, it's time to start listening to a different message from the one your busy brain was telling you back in your early teens. Remember, that audience you're worried about is imaginary. People are not looking at you or talking about you nearly as much as it feels like they are or felt like they were back then. You have so much to offer the world that only you can give. Don't hide it just because you're worried about what other people *might be* saying or thinking.

You are uniquely made in the image of God—with talents and passions and strengths that will make a difference to the world. We promise. But in order to start experiencing that difference, you first have to believe it's there.

Relationships

What it meant then: We asked a bunch of girls who are between 11 and 14 what they wish they knew about friendships. You probably thought about some of the same issues when you were their age. Here's what they said:

- Why do so many girls assume the friendship is over after a fight? Why can't they try to work it out?
- Why does it seem (especially with girls) that you are best friends one week and enemies the next?
- What is a good way to make new friends when you are at a new school?
- How do I deal with cliques in school?
- Why do girls gossip about each other?
- Why do girls act differently toward you when they are around guys?
- Why do some girls exclude others from their group?
- Why do really close friends act one way when they are with you and another way when they are with other friends?
- Why are girls jealous of other girls' success?

Relationships. Mean girls. Drama. They were part of your everyday life back then. Do you remember how you felt? Do you remember who was the meanest of the mean girls? It could have even been you. Whatever your position on the girl food chain might have been, you wondered about the same thing as every other girl: How do I find friends I can trust?

What it means now: As hard as those years were, you learned a lot of important lessons about relationships. You learned:

- What it felt like to be on the outside—because no matter

how many friends you had, you sometimes felt like you were all alone.

- What a friend is *not*—because all of us had at least one friend in junior high who talked behind our back, tried to steal our other friends, or was just mean.
- How important friends are. God made you to long for relationships with people who encourage, love, and support you. You learned this lesson from how bad it felt when you didn't have those relationships and how great it felt when you did.
- What it takes to be a friend. Relationships in your junior high years were filled with drama. Girls hurt each other's feelings daily—probably hourly. You undoubtedly got hurt and likely did your share of hurting others, too.

These are hard lessons to learn. But the good news is that you *did* learn them. You have the wisdom to avoid the misunderstandings and games that caused problems between you and your friends in junior high. You have the maturity to figure out how to mend a damaged friendship. And you have the confidence to stick with the friends who like you for who you are. So use all of that to love the friends God has put in your life. It will be a tremendous gift to them—and to you.

The High Points

*Suddenly or gradually, we were confronted with the fact
that not only is life outside of us very complicated but life
inside of us is just as complicated, or even more so.*

— *Henri Nouwen,* Intimacy

Every summer at camp we have a different theme. Unlike some camps, we don't come up with this theme months ahead of time. I (Melissa) am more of a wait-and-see kind of girl. I have to be with the kids so I can see who they are and what they need. Then I like to figure out what we have to work with. We often use simple, everyday objects to talk about God; the kind that remind you of God wherever you are, whatever you're doing. We've used everything from cups to clay pots to pancakes to bring Scripture to life for our campers. We've even used a toilet for a camp of second through fourth graders. That certainly got their attention.

One summer we had a lot of extra bread. Panera Bread donates bread to our ministry once a week, and we bring it to camp. We are so grateful—and so up to our ears in bread. That summer after my wait-and-see period was over, I decided to go with what was available—bread. The talks I gave using bread that summer had a lot to do with the high points of being an 11-to-14-year-old girl.

In Luke 24:13-34 there is a story about two men walking to the town of Emmaus. This happened a few days after Jesus' death on the cross. The two men had no idea Jesus had been raised from the dead. So they were walking and talking about how sad they were that Jesus had died. Then Jesus himself came along and asked them what they'd been talking about. They were shocked this guy didn't know the story and proceeded to tell him all about Jesus. Jesus responded by telling them the history behind the story and how his death was predicted and talked about all the way through the Bible. But he never told them who he was.

It started getting dark, and the two travelers convinced Jesus to stay the night with them rather than continuing on his journey. He agreed and started handing out bread. And that's when the story changes. Luke writes, "When he was at the table with them, he took bread, gave thanks, broke it and began to give it to them. Then their eyes were opened and they recognized him" (Luke 24:30-31).

Clearly, this is not a story about teenage girls. But a lot in this story reminds us of some of the great things that happen in girls between the ages of 11 and 14. Here are the high points about bread we discussed at camp that summer.

Hunger

What it meant then: The story of Jesus and these two men includes a kind of repeat of the Last Supper (when Jesus broke bread and passed it around to his disciples). That's why the two men recognized Jesus while they were eating. What's so interesting about this part of the story is how ordinary it is. It's not like Jesus performed a miracle to show who he was. He did the most normal thing in the world—he shared bread (which is the symbol of his life) with them.

There are several places in the Bible where bread is used

to talk about Jesus' life and his goodness (take a look at Matthew 4:4, Matthew 6:1, Matthew 14:13-18). And it also talks about hunger and thirst as metaphors for our need for God (see Matthew 5:6). That's what we wanted to talk about with our campers—the hunger girls start to feel in junior high.

When you were little, life seemed pretty easy. But as you got older and your awareness started to kick in, you noticed that your parents didn't get along sometimes. You were hurt by people who were supposed to be your friends. You hurt the people you loved. Life just didn't make sense the way it used to, and you began to want a sense of purpose in your life.

At the end of each camp we ask the campers a few very important questions:

- How many of you would like to have a relationship with Christ?
- How many of you feel far away from him but would like to be closer?
- How many of you want your life to make a difference for God?

It's always exciting to see all the hands shoot up and, year after year, most of the hands belong to fifth through eighth graders. The funny thing is that the kids who raise their hands also raised their hands the year before and the year before that—often for the same questions. Kids from 11 to 14 are spiritually hungry—hungry for the kind of life and goodness Jesus offers. They know their lives are complicated, and they want someone bigger to be in charge. They want to have a real relationship with God. And they're so hungry they want that relationship year after year after year.

When Jesus sat down to eat with those two men and took the bread in his hands, it was a reminder to them—and to us—that he has also taken our lives in his hands. Just as Jesus knew how to meet physical hunger with bread, he can meet our spiritual hunger with his love, his truth, and his grace.

What it means now: When you were in junior high, that hunger for something more was intense. Now that you're older, schedules, relationships, and life in general crowd out that hunger. It's harder to spend time focusing on prayer because you have so much on your mind. You're up late doing homework and that makes it tough to get to the Bible study that meets before school. You can't always make it to youth group because you've got practice that night. But even in the middle of all that busyness, you feel the hunger to stay close to God.

Use this hunger to find new ways to connect with Jesus. Talk to him when you're driving to school. Read your Bible while you eat breakfast. Plan a Bible study with a few friends that will work with your schedules. And share your time and talents with other people. Help out in the church nursery. Go on a mission trip. Pay attention to your hunger for God, and fill yourself with his grace and goodness.

Messiness

What it meant then: I (Sissy) was a pretty good kid. I was the kind of kid adults really liked—even in those awkward years between 11 and 14. I was able to convince them that I was the whole package—kind, respectful, polite, thoughtful. But I knew there were other parts of me, too—the parts I kept hidden on the inside.

Don't get me wrong. I didn't have a secret life where I was snorting cocaine or sleeping with lots of different guys. But there were things I didn't like about myself that to me felt just about as awful. I didn't like how I treated people when I got angry. I didn't like the thoughts I had toward certain people at school. I didn't like how emotionally needy I felt at times. Even though I looked pretty good on the outside, I knew I was a mess on the inside.

It was probably during your junior high years you first became aware of your messiness. It could be that you were really nice to everyone at school but came home and unleashed on your parents. Maybe the way you talked to boys in person was very different from the way you talked to them on the Internet. Only you know for sure, but we would guess there was some part of you that was a little messier than the part you presented to the world.

What it means now: As hard as this knowledge can be, it's an important part of growing up. An author we really like named Richard Rohr says you start to truly become yourself when you realize two things:
- The world doesn't work the way you think it should.
- You don't work the way you think you should.

In other words life doesn't always turn out the way you expect—people disappoint you, you don't get the recognition or credit you know you've earned, you aren't valued or respected for who you are.

But the second part of Rohr's statement is just as powerful because as much as you want to do the right thing, there will be times when you don't do it. You'll yell at someone for no reason. You'll forget something important and hurt someone's feelings or ruin a big project. You'll overreact and say something mean. You will feel like a mess.

Here's the great news: Jesus knows you're a mess and he loves you. He doesn't even love you in spite of the mess—he just loves you, mess and all. Remember the story of Jesus and those men? He took the bread and broke it—bread is only edible when it's broken. In the same way—with great kindness and mercy—Jesus breaks through our pride and efforts to put on a perfect image. And once you accept that you aren't perfect you can stop being afraid to be yourself. You can admit when you've messed up, apologize, and seek forgiveness from God and the people you've hurt. And then you can start over. You live and love and take risks and mess up and look for grace again, knowing that you are loved just the way you are.

Awareness

What it meant then: These years between 11 and 14 are filled with irony dressed in teenage clothes. You're saying "come close" and "get away" at the same time. You're desperate for relationships but afraid to let people see who you truly are. You are consumed with yourself but just beginning to realize there are other people in the world. The author Madeleine L'Engle wrote, "And that was my moment of awareness: that woman across the court who did not know me, and whom I did not know, was a person. She had thoughts of her own. She was. Our lives would never touch. I would never know her name. And yet it was she who revealed to me my first glimpse of personhood." (L'Engle, 33)

This awareness that Madeleine L'Engle described is the kind that began when you were in your early teens. Other people exist. They think and feel and have needs. As much as you were consumed with what *you* thought and felt and needed, you were also waking up to the thoughts and feelings and needs of others.

What it means now: Your awareness probably started small. It was focused mostly on your friends and other kids your age. A friend told you she was worried about her parents getting a divorce, you noticed a girl crying in the bathroom at school, you felt bad for the guy in your class who got picked on every day at lunch. You knew those people were hurting and you wanted to help. But you still weren't aware that your parents had feelings or needs that didn't have anything to do with you, or that the strangers you passed on the street had struggles, too.

Now you're more aware of the needs of people inside and outside your daily life. Even though you still yell at your sister sometimes, you know that it hurts her feelings and you work to make up with her. You realize that when your mom is sad it doesn't necessarily mean you've done something wrong. And you also recognize how important it is to help people who are hurting—whether it's the girl who sits next to you in school or the family living in a cardboard shack on the other side of the world. You're becoming aware that you can make a tremendous difference.

Puberty

What it meant then: Believe it or not, puberty is one of the high points of these years. But it doesn't feel that way when you're going through it. I (Melissa) recently talked to a girl named Brittney who had just started her period. She said, "Everyone told me that becoming a woman was so important—that I should be really excited about it. I started my period and it has been a nightmare! I mean what's so great about it? You don't feel good. You have to deal with tampons and pads and all of that. It doesn't feel so important to me. It just feels like a pain!"

The impact of puberty can feel like it's a pretty big low point. In his book, *The Wonder of Girls*, psychologist Michael Gurian lists all the ways periods affect girls during puberty:

- Your moods
- The words you use, the speed of your conversation, your need for conversation

- How you do on tests when you're having or about to have your period
- How much you eat
- How you relate to people nonverbally (without saying a word)
- How you feel about the people you love
- How you see yourself fitting in
- Your self-esteem
- Your desire to make friends
- Emotions such as anger, joy, and sadness (Gurian, 78-79)

Sounds pretty overwhelming, doesn't it? It was when you went through puberty. Your hormones were basically in the driver's seat of your whole world. And because it took a while for your period to become regular, it took a while for your hormones to settle down, too.

What it means now: Your body has finally become a little more predictable. Yes, your hormones will still wreak havoc on you in the days right around your period. And they will when you're an adult, too. But now you know that your lousy mood, your tiredness, and your increased sensitivity to other people doesn't mean your life is terrible. You know these feelings will pass in a few days. You've learned not to take those hurt feelings quite so seriously and to give yourself—and others—a break.

As your hormones take over every month, you might feel a little like Brittney and wonder, "What's the point?" But on other days you realize all that puberty craziness was part of becoming a woman. And being a woman is a great thing. Your hunger and awareness are growing into gifts of intuition and compassion and tenderness and strength. You've been given a tremendous gift in your ability to have children—that's the point of having a period, after all (even though that's *way* down the road). You simply wouldn't be the woman you will be one day without puberty, your period, and the gifts they bring with them.

By the way, Brittney, the girl who just started her period, has a six-year-old sister. Brittney and her family agreed that her little sister wasn't quite ready to learn about periods—and all the paraphernalia that comes with them—yet. One night Brittney was baby-sitting her sister and her sister's friend. She heard strange noises and went upstairs to check on the girls. Her sister had not only discovered Brittney's pads, but she and her friend had attached them to the bottoms of their feet and were sliding down the hall on them. She looked at Brittney and said, "Brittney, are these things yours?"

The years between 11 and 14 are filled with rough spots. But a lot of good comes out of those years, too. Now that you're through them, you can see all the ways you have changed and grown and become more of who you were created to be.

The story of Jesus' visit with the two men ends at the table. He took the bread, broke it, and gave it to them. And it was not until that moment they realized he was Jesus. They recognized him.

Now that you're older, you can recognize some of the highest high points of being an 11-to-14-year-old. And they just get higher as you get older. You can have a hunger for Christ that is even stronger than it was in those early years. You can recognize the brokenness and messiness of your own life and allow Jesus to use it to show God's love to others. You can see the needs of other people and show them love, patience, and compassion.

God created you to make a difference in the world. The hunger, messiness, and awareness that started growing in you during your junior high years is only becoming more of who you are. And they combine to help you reflect Christ to the world in a way no one else can.

Low Points

Adolescent girls are like saplings in a hurricane.
They are young and vulnerable trees that the winds
blow with gale strength. — Mary Pipher, Reviving Ophelia

You're in the car on your way to the beach—and you've been there for quite some time. Your legs are restless, you're thirsty, and you have to go to the bathroom. Your little brother is playing very loud video games. Your dad is singing oldies with the radio. Your mom is sleeping—and snoring. You're bored and ready to be wherever it is you're going.

We think being 15 and 16 years old is a lot like the "are-we-there-yet?" feeling you used to get (and maybe still do) on road trips. You're always waiting for the next exciting thing.

Fifteen is a quick stopover. It's pretty much all about getting your learner's permit, waiting to turn 16, and being in high school. Sure, 15 is fun, but you're convinced it's not nearly as great as 16 is going to be.

And then you hit it. You're 16. You get to drive. You have freedom! It is thrilling—for a while. Then you start thinking about how much better life will be when you're 17. And you can't even imagine what it will be like at 18.

We want to encourage you to consider slowing down a little. There *are* exciting times to come. There is so much stirring inside of you. But we don't want you to be so focused on those times you miss all the wonderful moments of growing up that are part of your life right now.

During these years you will build friendships, have experiences, and make discoveries about yourself that will be essential parts of your life from this point on. The high points of these years are better than you can imagine—and we'll get to those in the next chapter. There will be low points, too. But as you've probably noticed, those low points help you find out who you are just as much—and sometimes more—than the high points. Allow the hard parts of being 15 and 16 to be something God uses to help you know him—and yourself— even better.

Peer pressure

Peer pressure—or at least the way most girls think adults think about peer pressure—is a myth. We often have girls tell us, "I don't feel peer pressure. None of my friends would ever tell me I have to drink or smoke." These girls think peer pressure looks like one friend holding a beer bottle out to another saying, "I won't be your friend unless you take a drink," or passing the pot and saying, "Come on, try it. Everyone else is."

We're not really sure how that mythical version of peer pressure got started, but we know it is not the kind of pressure you really experience. Your friends aren't trying to get you drunk or high—and if they are, they're definitely not the kind of friends you need. But a lot of girls face a different kind of pressure. It's subtle and unspoken, but it's just as powerful.

Not long ago I (Sissy) met with a girl named Beth. Beth was grounded because she'd been riding in a car with a group of friends when the police pulled them over. The guy driving the car had been drinking and there was a cooler of beer in the trunk. Beth hadn't been drinking at all. She ended up in the car because she needed a ride home from a party. She knew the driver had been drinking, but he assured her he was in perfect shape to drive. Beth considered driving herself but she didn't have a license. She wasn't sure which decision would be worse—illegal driving or riding with a driver who'd been drinking. She took her chances and got in the back seat of the car.

The driver ended up spending the night in jail and facing charges for DUI and supplying alcohol to minors. The other kids have court dates coming up and will either be sent to juvenile detention or put on probation with loads of community service hours. Beth was the only one who hadn't been drinking, so she avoided legal problems. But her parents were very upset.

Beth told me, "Every party I go to has alcohol. I don't know what to do. I am the only one of my friends who doesn't drink. I don't want to drink—it's just not worth it. But it's so hard not to when everyone else is."

This is what true peer pressure looks like. Like Beth, you might find that your friends aren't really trying to convince you to do something you don't want to do. They're just doing it and it feels lonely and almost dorky to be the only one who isn't.

As I talked with Beth, I tried to encourage her to consider hanging out with some different people. If you've been in a situation like hers, I'd suggest the same to you. We know there are probably a lot of kids at your school who drink and smoke—and do a whole lot of other things that could get them into a lot of trouble. But there are also kids who don't. Really. In every school. Find those kids.

As you can see from Beth's story, you don't have to do anything obviously wrong to lose your parents' trust or get in trouble with the law. If you're hanging around with people who are involved in anything illegal—whether it's underage drinking or smoking or even sneaking out and taking the car—it's only a matter of time before you suffer the consequences of being around all of that stuff. Stay away from it—or at least those people when they're doing it. Nothing is worth losing your parents' trust. Just ask someone who has learned the hard way:

Finding out who you are is a huge part of being a teenager. When I was starting high school, I got caught up in that and headed in the wrong direction. I was starting to find out people can let you down, and I wanted to ease the pain. I wanted to find something that wouldn't let me down, something that would make me feel good, make me not think about all the disappointment. I started using drugs and drinking and quickly found out it made me stop feeling anything. I was that person who made things look fun and easy, but inside I was falling apart. I was trying to walk away from real life and I got lost.

When I was using drugs and caught up in the lifestyle that went with that, I wasn't living in a fun or happy way. My life was full of pain. Now I know that's because I wasn't living the way God wanted me to live. I was running from him.

I wish I'd known I was strong enough to make better decisions. I want you to know that you can make those decisions, too. You have unique strength and beauty that God has placed inside of you. And most importantly, I want to tell you that if you ask him, God will give you the power to make the decisions that lead you toward the life he calls you to.—Mary Ann, 19

Drinking, drugs, sex—none of these things are worth the trouble they cause. They just hurt you. You will enjoy life so much more when you don't have to lie to your parents, when you spend time with people without worrying about getting into trouble, when you aren't trying to be someone you know you're not. Sometimes it can feel like you're the only one trying to stay away from alcohol and drugs. But trust us, you're not. Other people at your school are trying to make good decisions based on what they believe God wants them to do. Find those people and watch how much fun and freedom you can have when you're making decisions your parents would be proud of and you can feel good about, too.

And don't forget what Mary Ann said about Jesus. He dealt with some pretty tough temptations himself and trusted God in the midst of it (Matthew 4:1-11). God wants to give you a confidence, joy, and peace nothing else can even touch.

Rules

"I have the strictest parents in the world!" You can't imagine how many times we've heard that statement from the girls who come to Daystar. You may have even said those words yourself. Clearly, rules often feel like one of the very lowest low points of being 15 and 16. Maybe one of these statements sounds familiar to you:

- "It doesn't make sense for Caroline to bring me home that early. Her curfew is a whole hour later. Why can't I stay out until she has to go home?"
- "I can't believe you won't let me see that movie. Every single person in my grade has already seen it—half of them with their parents!"
- "Everyone else has been dating for two years. I'm way more mature than half of them. Why won't you let me date?"
- "I'm a good kid. If I were a bad kid, all these rules would make sense."
- "When will you ever start trusting me?"

We would guess you have said (or thought) at least one of these at some point in the last year or two. You're in—or almost in—high school. You want to be independent. You believe you're trustworthy, but your parents aren't sure, even if you've never been in trouble. But in spite of that, your parents most likely have one or two rules you wish didn't exist.

This whole idea of trust is one of the biggest reasons girls your age argue with their parents. Every rule feels like one more way they refuse to trust you. But we want to let you in on a little secret about parents and trust. It's not that your parents don't trust you, it's that they don't trust everyone else. They don't trust the other drivers on the streets late at night. They don't trust the boys they don't know. (They probably don't trust the ones they do know, either). They don't trust other parents they haven't met. What looks like a lack of trust in you is really their attempt at protecting you from the dangers they know are out there. Even though it doesn't always feel like it, the rules are a sign of their love.

We asked a group of high school girls what they know now that they wish they had known when they were younger. One girl responded, "I wish I had known that when your parents say you can't do something or go somewhere or shouldn't watch or listen to certain things, it's not because they want to make your life miserable. It's because they are looking out for you and want what's best for you."

We knew this girl when she was 15; she was one of those girls who believed her parents were the strictest parents on the planet. As a matter of fact, almost every girl we talked to eventually realized that her parents were right about a lot.

So maybe while you're complaining about your parents and wanting them to trust you, you can start to trust them a little more, too. You might find when you stop pushing the boundaries, they begin to widen on their own.

The need to belong

Kristy was 16 the first time she saw a counselor. Her parents thought she needed counseling. She didn't think so. She said everything was fine. But when football games rolled around on the weekends, Kristy didn't have anyone to go with. She hadn't been invited to birthday parties, dances, or get-togethers of any kind in several years. Her parents were worried, so they did what many concerned parents do—brought her in to talk to someone.

After his first session with Kristy, her counselor invited her parents into his office. "I really don't think Kristy needs to be here. She told me about her life and how you are worried that she doesn't have many friends. I think Kristy is just different. I think she's content to be by herself. Kristy doesn't seem to need friends as much as some other girls her age."

What's your reaction when you read this counselor's words? Here's what we think: Baloney! We haven't met a girl yet—and between us we've counseled over 10,000 of them— who doesn't desperately desire relationships. Some of them just put up a good front.

Let us show you a journal entry from another girl we know. She wrote, "I don't feel like I belong here. I'm not sure I belong anywhere. I don't have any friends. Even my best friend has turned her back on me. What have I done to deserve all of this? Do they think I'm mean? Too ugly? Too fat? Will I ever feel important to anyone again?" This girl was a lot like Kristy. On the outside she seemed perfectly content being by herself. If we'd asked her about it, she would have told us she was fine. She never would have admitted the feelings she wrote about in her journal. But regardless of how she acted, she had an intense need to belong.

So do you. So do we. It's a normal part of how God designed us. Remember all that brain stuff we talked about? But that need looks different at 15 and 16 than it did in junior high. Back then it was really important to belong to a group, to be seen with and included by certain people. Now being in a group isn't quite enough. You want to be important to someone. You want a best friend—or at least a few really close friends. You may want a boyfriend. You might have all of these relationships already. Or you might be hoping and praying they'll come along soon.

Life can be hard when you don't have relationships where you feel important. It can be lonely. And it can make you start to doubt yourself. Like the girl whose journal entry you read, you might start to believe you've done something to cause the loneliness you feel, that there's something wrong with you. Please believe us when we say that there isn't. You are likable and enjoyable and worthy of love and friendship, no matter who you are.

Turning your loneliness in on yourself is one of the worst ways to deal with this feeling. It only makes you feel worse about yourself, which makes you want to avoid people, which just makes you more lonely. We know so many girls who feel lonely, so they sit at home, all alone, feeing sad about how lonely they are. Guess what happens? They keep feeling lonely because they're at home, all alone. If you feel like you don't belong anywhere try looking in new places. Go to your youth group. Get involved with a club at school. Start playing a sport. Ask the girl who smiles at you at lunch if you can sit with her. We know it's a risk but you are well worth the effort.

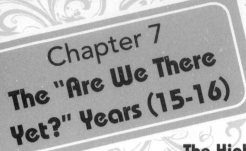

The High Points

*At the same time Much-Afraid herself was conscious of a
wonderful stirring in her own heart, as though something
were springing up and breaking into new life there, too.*
— *Hannah Hurnard,* Hinds' Feet on High Places

When I (Sissy) was 16, I almost died on a ski trip. It wasn't
what you might think. I didn't hit a tree or fall off a ski lift.
I—along with seven of my best friends—got carbon monoxide poisoning.

We were on a youth group trip at a camp in Colorado. The
heating system in our cabin malfunctioned and we breathed
in carbon monoxide for several hours while we were asleep.
When we woke up, each of us showed different symptoms.
Angie thought another friend of ours was her mom. Tami
passed out on the bathroom floor trying to take a pill. Jenny
couldn't see herself in the mirror. And I thought I had really
bad period cramps. When one of our friends went to the next
cabin to get help, all she could say before she fell to the floor
was, "We all have headaches."

It turns out the stages of carbon monoxide poisoning are
headache, nausea, hysteria, coma, death. I think we hit all of
the first three. We later learned that we were within an hour
of dying. It was a traumatic experience for our youth group
and our families.

But my memory is not one of trauma. It's kind of like Melissa and the merry-go-round incident. What stays with me are funny things about that day, like how Grace Ann stood up and told someone to plug in her rollers and then fell immediately back on the bed.

Maybe what I remember most is what happened afterward. Obviously, we didn't ski that day. We stayed behind and had lunch by ourselves in the dining hall. I remember that a worship song we loved was playing on the radio and we sat at a round table crying and praying together about how grateful we were to be alive.

It was a powerful spiritual experience I'll never forget. And that's my strongest memory. The low points were there, but the feeling I remember is thankfulness. I felt a sense of belonging, not only to an amazing group of friends, but also to a God who loved and protected me. God used a low point to teach me about strength and to show me the depth of his love for me. He showed me I could trust in the hugeness of his grace. And grace is what so much of the high points of 15 and 16 are all about.

The end of hiccups

Your confidence was in pretty short supply in those junior high years. The hiccups in confidence we talked about made it next to impossible to feel good about yourself—at least for any stretch of time. But when you're 15 and 16, your brain growth slows down again and the hiccups stop. You're able to find a little more confidence in who you are instead of only frustration in who you're not.

It can be hard for girls to show their confidence. We get really worried about coming across as stuck up or arrogant. So instead, we act like we don't know as much as we do, or

like we aren't as talented as we are. You might remember the girls in elementary school who bragged about everything they did or the girls you know now who flaunt what they have. And you know you don't want to be anything like that.

But there is a big difference between arrogance and confidence. Arrogance is valuing yourself *above* others. Confidence is valuing yourself *among* others.

We have a friend about your age who comes across as very confident, but not for the reasons you might suspect. She's not a fantastic singer or a great writer or a talented artist or a champion athlete or a star student, although she does all of those things. But she's not a rock star in any of those areas where we assume people find confidence. Instead, her confidence comes from a much deeper place.

She has an inner confidence in who she is and who she is becoming. She has a humble confidence, mostly because she takes what she has been given and shares it with others. She spends a lot of time with a family of four young children who don't have much of a relationship with their mom. She talks to her grandmother often and lets her know how important she is. She has raised several thousand dollars for Daystar by going around her school and neighborhood asking for donations for kids who can't afford counseling. There is nothing arrogant about her, but she is confident because she knows her life makes a difference to others. The bottom line is that she believes God has begun something good in her (Philippians 1:6), and she knows from experience that this goodness gets much richer when she shares it with others.

The end of narcissism
Realizing not everything is about you helps get rid of some of that intense pressure you felt a few years ago. You figure out you

don't have to look or act a certain way to have friends. You're free to be who you really are instead of some "I-want-to-be-popular-so-I'd-better-try-to-be-like-everyone-else" version of yourself.

But the best part of moving beyond narcissism is you're free to care about the people around you. When everything stops coming through the "all-about-me" filter, you realize there's a lot going on in the lives of others that has nothing to do with you.

Remember when you were 12 or 13 and one of your friends would be kind of quiet at lunch? Your first question was usually, "Are you mad at me?" Any strange behavior from any friend meant she was upset with you or possibly didn't even want to be your friend anymore. That's the "all-about-me" filter at work.

Now your questions are more along the lines of "What's wrong?" or "Are you okay?" You realize that your friend's feelings likely have nothing to do with you. She might be quiet because she got in a fight with her mom on the way to school. Or her boyfriend broke up with her. Or her parents aren't getting along so well. Now that the narcissism has faded, you can listen to your friend without thinking about yourself. You can show her you care because you're no longer worried about how she feels about you at the moment.

Convictions

We've already talked about the whole peer pressure thing. It's happening to every girl your age to some degree. It could be pressure to drink, to sneak out, to take your parents' car, to lie about your homework, to cheat on a test, or any one of a million things the people around you are doing. We know they're not necessarily telling you to do those things, but they're doing them—and making it look pretty cool and consequence-free.

So now it's time for you to decide. All the "Just say no" ads in the world can't actually say no for you when it comes time to choose. You have to decide what kind of person you want to be. You have to decide what kind of relationship you want with your parents—one where they trust you or one where you have to lie to them and cover up what you're doing.

A lot of the teenagers we see in our offices are drinking—or lying to their parents, or doing all kinds of other things that could get them in trouble. They are usually doing these things as a reaction to something else. Their parents make them mad, so they do whatever their parents don't want them to do. They think they're rejecting their parents' choices and choosing for themselves. But they're not. They are just as controlled by their parents as if they were doing exactly what their parents told them to do.

Here's what we mean. Hope's mom tells her she doesn't want her hanging out with Jennifer anymore. Hope doesn't even like Jennifer that much. She knows Jennifer isn't very trustworthy and that she's a bad influence. But when Hope's mom says she doesn't want Hope to spend time with Jennifer, Hope decides that Jennifer is going to be her new best friend.

You see, Hope isn't choosing Jennifer because she really likes her and wants to hang out with her. She's choosing Jennifer as a reaction to her mom. So Hope's mom is still determining Hope's choices.

This happens more than you can imagine—with everything from friends to boys to curfews to drugs to alcohol. But these girls aren't making their own decisions. They aren't even necessarily making the decisions they want to make. They are making the decisions they think their parents *don't* want them to make.

We want something different for you. We want you to truly choose—not just react. We want you to think about who you want to be, how you want other people to see you, who you believe God created you to be. Then we want you to act like that person. It will be hard at times. But God will never let you be tempted beyond what you can handle. The Bible says, "No temptation has overtaken you except what is common to us all. And God is faithful; he will not let you be tempted beyond what you can bear. But when you are tempted, he will also provide a way out so that you can endure it" (1 Corinthians 10:13).

Last fall, when our regular counseling groups started up again for the school year, one of the girls, Leigh Ann, came in as confident as we had ever seen her. Each of the girls talked about what they wanted for themselves during the year. Leigh Ann said she wanted to be a godly example. She said so many of her friends think of Christians as judgmental and negative. She wanted to show them something different. She wanted to show them Christ—to love them with joy, integrity, and humility.

This kind of change in who you are and who you can be starts with that simple act of wanting to be different. Leigh Ann has moved out of narcissism. Her hiccups are over. She is committed to learning and growing even when she messes up. She wants to continue in this good work God began inside of her. And she is ready to make the kind of choices that will lead her in that direction.

Chapter 8
The Independent—More or Less— Years (17-19)

The Low Points

I no more knew who I was then than in most ways I know who I am now, but I knew that I could survive more or less on my own in more or less the real world.

— *Frederick Buechner,* The Sacred Journey

This is it! The years you've been waiting for are finally here and you—you don't know what to think. The end of your teenage years is filled with mixed emotions. You finally feel like you've grown up, but you aren't sure you're ready to face life on your own. You can't wait to head into whatever your plans are after high school, but you hate the idea of leaving your friends—and them leaving you. You are actually starting to enjoy the adults in your life again and realizing your days of living with them are coming to a close.

If you feel a little of that familiar ambivalence during these years, you're not alone. We asked some of our 17-, 18-, and 19-year-old Facebook friends what they thought about this time in their lives. Here's what they had to say:

What are the best parts of being 17-19?
- Having a driver's license
- Making new friends
- So much more freedom
- Staying out later

- Hanging with your friends
- Dating
- Feeling like you know yourself
- Finally being independent
- Being more of a friend with my mom
- Feeling like my friendships are stable

What are the hardest parts of being 17-19?
- Feeling capable (and being so close) to independence but knowing you still are under the authority of your parents
- The relationship thing with boys
- The transition between having your life laid out for you and laying out your own future
- Having your heart broken for the first time
- Being ready for college but still having to tell your parents where you're going and who you're going with
- Wanting your parents to recognize you as an adult

Do you see a common theme in these statements about the hard part of being 17, 18, and 19? What would your answers be? Most of theirs (and probably yours) have to do with being caught between life as a teenager and life as an adult. You want freedom and responsibility—at least some responsibility. You want to go where you want, when you want, and not have to report home when your plans change at the last minute. You are emotionally ready for more mature relationships but your ex-boyfriend wasn't.

Most girls this age feel like the high points are even higher than they were before. That's partly because of your increasing independence and partly because of your maturity level—you are truly becoming your own person.

But girls also find the low points are lower. You may be much more mature than your boyfriend—who would rather play PS2 than take you out on a date. One girl also told us this was the age when she realized the limits of some of her friendships. "I knew I could expect things from certain friends and not from others." The various maturity levels of the people around you can be really frustrating—especially if you are one of the more mature people in your group of friends. We find that a lot of girls are tired of playing relationship games by the time they hit 17 and 18—games their friends still want to play. And that leads to some definite low points.

You might also find yourself frustrated that this independent person you are becoming is still subject to your parents' rules. You feel so ready to make your own decisions, live your own life, and yet you still have to answer to someone. It can feel like you'll never be treated like an adult. Clearly, as great as these years are, there are still some pretty significant low points for 17-to-19-year-olds.

Body image

Have you heard of the "freshman 15"? It's not the first 15 friends you make at college, it's the 15 pounds almost every freshman gains during his or her first year of school. It happens for all kinds of reason, including:

1) Ordering pizza at 2 a.m.
2) No more high school sports
3) The end of puberty
4) More pizza at 2 a.m.

There are some obvious ways to avoid this situation—stick to some healthy eating habits, keep the pizza to a once-a-week treat, get some exercise a few times a week. Or you can just not worry about it and know your weight will level out eventually. But we find that most girls are thrown by this sudden change in their bodies. Girls who haven't worried much about their weight wonder what on earth is happening to them. And girls who have worried about their weight for years feel like they have totally lost the battle to stay at a weight they feel good about.

The freshman 15 isn't just the result of all that pizza. A number of changes are taking place in your body—and your life—that combine to change the way your body looks and feels.

The primary change is that all those wild and wacky puberty hormones are slowing down. That means your metabolism is slowing down, too. Your body burns calories more slowly and stores fat that it used to flush out. So in these late teen years, your body settles into its postpuberty size. Your arms get a little wider, as do your legs and bottom. Your stomach might start to hang over your low-waisted jeans, and your sweaters might get a little tighter in the chest area. Developing these curves is all part of being a woman.

Our culture has forgotten that curves are beautiful and normal. Not so long ago, the women considered the most beautiful had serious curves. Go online and look for pictures of Marilyn Monroe or Sophia Loren. These women were famous for their beauty and their figures. Take a look at Judy Garland in *The Wizard of Oz*. Her 16-year-old body looks pretty different from those of the teenagers you see in the media today.

During the 1960s, the fashion industry decided to shake up the way people thought about beauty and moved from using curvy models to using thin—almost too thin—models like Twiggy (her nickname tells you a lot!). It's important to remember that Twiggy and other stick-thin models were meant to shock the audience. They were intended to look so unlike "regular" women that they would grab the attention of anyone looking at the clothing advertisement. In other words, these super-skinny models weren't supposed to look like the rest of us—and we weren't supposed to look like them.

Now—thanks to computers—even the models themselves don't look like their pictures. Photographers and magazine designers can fix every flaw on a model's face so her skin looks perfect in print even if she had a huge pimple on the day of the photo shoot. They can manipulate the size of her hips, the length of her legs, and the shape of her arms to make her look thinner and more toned than she is—or than anyone ever could be. The look so many magazines sell you doesn't even exist.

Maybe you've heard it before, but it never hurts to hear it again: Curves are beautiful! And don't worry about what guys will think if you put on a few pounds and go up a pants size. Most guys like girls with a few curves.

Nearly every girl will gain weight during these years. You are becoming a woman, and women don't look like 12-year-olds. You are beautiful. And, as you will hear us say through-out this book, your beauty has much more to do with who you are than how much you weigh.

Sex and confusion

The physical part of your relationship with boys has the po-tential to get really confusing in these years. Maybe it already has. You've probably noticed that you think about boys in a whole different way than you did when you were 13 or 15 or even 16. Not long ago, boys were just weird and irritating. Then you started noticing which ones were nice—and cute. You had friends who started "going out" or "going with" or "dating"—or whatever the term was at your school for talking on the phone once a week, but avoiding each other in the halls. In junior high, boyfriends were more about status than the intimacy of relationship. But that changes when you are 17 and 18.

Now it's becoming important to connect—really connect—with someone. You want to be significant. You want someone to care about you, to call you and send you flowers and take you out on dates and tell you you're beautiful. You want to feel emotionally close to the guys you date.

Not only do you want to connect emotionally with boys, but your body is starting to tell you it wants to connect with boys, too. You've probably noticed that more of the girls your age are talking about sex—who's had it, who hasn't, who is doing what with whom. Maybe some of your friends have had sex. Maybe you have, too. All of this talk about sex can change your perspective on guys and dating. But it also can change the way you think about yourself.

Last year I (Melissa) met with a girl who'd had sex for the first time. She was a little older than you. She was a Christian and had promised herself she wouldn't have sex until she got married. But she was in love and she got confused. The guy she was dating was very sweet—he was a Christian, too—and told her it was okay because they were going to get married one day. They hadn't been dating long when they had sex. And they didn't date much longer.

He hung around for maybe another month and then broke up with her. Actually he just started avoiding her and acting weird. She was left with no boyfriend, a broken promise to herself and God, and a whole lot of guilt.

"I think the real reason I had sex with him is because I didn't have a reason not to," she told me. "I knew God said you are supposed to wait until you get married, but I really thought he was the one. I knew it was wrong but I thought it would be okay because I loved him. And as much as I hate to admit it, I knew God would forgive me, so why not do it?"

"What I didn't understand was *why* God said it was wrong. I thought it was more of a rule than a way of protecting me. Now I know that this is why God didn't want me to have sex before I was married. He knew I would end up feeling like this, sobbing because I gave something very important to someone who could walk away from me and never look back."

And that is precisely why. We cannot begin to tell you the hundreds—probably thousands—of girls who have come to us for counseling because their boyfriend—the one who had promised to never leave them—had broken up with them. They had sex with these boys for all kinds of reasons—he threatened to break up with me, I believed we were in love and would get married one day, I thought it would make him love me, I liked how it felt when he told me I was beautiful.

The ironic truth is that guys don't respect girls who sleep around. They don't stay with girls who are willing to have sex after a few dates. Lots of guys out there will say and do all the right things to get you to have sex with them, but they aren't the kind of guys who will want the kind of relationship you long for.

You want a guy who will treasure you for who you are, one who will respect you for your heart and your brains and your strength. You want a guy who will honor your courage when you stand up for what you believe. There are lots of guys like that out there. They might not be the most popular guys or the coolest guys or the ones every girl wants to date. But they are the ones who will treat you with the care and respect you deserve.

Of course it's not always the boys who are pushing for sex. The sex drive of girls doesn't get talked about much, but as you are well aware, girls want sex, too—or at least want the things leading up to sex. That can make it confusing and difficult to say no when a guy wants to have sex. All that kissing and touching triggers a physical response in girls—as well as in guys—that makes you want to keep going, to do all the things you know you shouldn't do.

We want you to know that your desire for sex is normal—it's a part of how God made you. But you can still say no. God created you to want sex, but he designed it to be part of marriage. So when God says no, it's not to torture you by keeping you from something he made you to want. It's *for your protection*. And as much as you might think it's no big deal, it is. There is something intimately spiritual about having sex, and it should be part of a relationship that isn't mixed with guilt.

If you have had sex, we want you to know that you can begin again. God forgives us and throws our sin into the depths of the sea (we'll talk more about that later). He forgets our sin completely. You can decide right now that you're not going to have sex with anyone else until you're married. God will honor that and honor you by helping you build guilt-free relationships.

The Bible shows us the way God wants us to live. It's easy to feel like it's just a long set of rules. But when things get confusing in the sex area (and they will), remember that God isn't about rules, God is about goodness. All the direction God gives us is meant to save us from heartache. He really does know best. He loves you and delights in you and wants you to have relationships in which you feel loved, respected, and valued. You will have those relationships and you can have them without all the guilt and pain that come from having sex outside of marriage.

Decisions, decisions!

Last year in our group for 11th and 12th-grade girls, one of the seniors said, "Do *not* ask me about college. If I have something to say, I'll tell you. I think I'll scream if one more person asks me where I'm going to school next year."

This is a stage of life that's filled with decisions. And with those decisions come all the questions: "What are you going to do after high school?" "Have you picked a college yet?" "What do you want to major in?" "Have you finished all your applications?" And on and on.

Your parents' friends and your relatives mean well. They don't realize that every other adult you've talked to in the last year (or three) has asked you the same questions. And they don't realize that every time you hear those questions, you are reminded of how huge these decisions feel.

Even when the big questions about what you're going to do after high school have been figured out, there are more decisions to be made. If you go to college, will you be in a sorority? Which one? Who will you room with? Which dorm will you live in? Will you work while you're in school? If you don't go to college, how are you going to make money? Should you keep living at home or get an apartment? Should you travel for a year? Join YWAM? Whew! Just writing about all these decisions is stressful—and reminds us how it felt to make them!

The real reason those questions are so frustrating is that they aren't just about your plans, they are about your life. You're trying to figure out what it's going to look like from this point on. Up until now it's all been pretty predictable— school, friends, family. But now that's about to change and you have to decide where you want to go, what you want to do, and who you want to be. The questions remind you of the huge amount of pressure you feel on a daily basis.

Listen to what one 19-year-old friend of ours had to say about the pressure she feels:

> The first semester of college has mostly been about me realizing I just can't get all of this right. There are so many people, phone calls, classes, work, projects, decisions, things to do all the time. I really thought I could manage my schedule perfectly and keep it all in line. But it's a struggle, which is teaching me deeper things about trust—trusting that God can give me the strength to get through the day. Trusting that I'll make it even if I can't get everything done or my days don't go the way I planned. I haven't exactly gotten that right yet, but I'm working on it.

Her words say just what we want you to know in the midst of all these decisions: You can't get it all right. There is no perfect future, no perfect job, no perfect college, no perfect sorority, definitely no perfect roommate. Making these decisions means you pray, trust God, decide, and then trust God some more. God has so many good things waiting out there for you. He says, "Forget the former things; do not dwell on the past. See, I am doing a new thing! Now it springs up; do you not perceive it? I am making a way in the wilderness and streams in the wasteland" (Isaiah 43:18-19). God is with you as you move into the future, making a way for you in the wilderness of all those decisions.

As you make your decisions, we want you to remember our friend's words. And we want you to remember to ask for help. Don't try making all of these choices on your own. Ask your parents or other adults you trust what they think. Take a career test. Spend some time with your college advisor. So many people would love to help—even if they drive you a little crazy with their questions.

I (Sissy) came home from that near-fatal ski trip with a sense of wonder and gratitude. Soon you'll feel that same way about these years. You'll learn to handle the pressure—the changes in your body, the changes in the way you see and want to connect with guys, and even the major changes going on in your life. God is doing a new thing. He is bringing new life into your life—even in the midst of the low points.

The High Points

Yet it is not our part to master all the tides of the world, but to
do what is in us for the succor of these years wherein we are set,
uprooting the evil in the fields that we know, so that those who
live after may have clean earth to till.

— *JRR Tolkien,* The Return of The King

Mastering tides would never have entered your mind when you were younger. You probably wouldn't have believed you could master much of anything. But today, after moving through the adventures of your younger years and the narcissism of your early teen years, you are starting to see that you can master quite a bit. That mastery is a big part of these independent years. You are talented and gifted and unique and you're finally starting to realize the impact you can make.

These years are full of high points. They are overflowing with idealism, purpose, and independence that can make you ready to conquer the world—or at least ready to "uproot the evil in the fields that you know," as Tolkien says. You can make a difference. And that is what this chapter—and this time—is all about.

Idealism

Anna was 17 when she first came to counseling. Her parents brought her because they were worried she was insecure. As

Anna sat in my (Melissa's) office, she told me what she wanted to do with her life.

"Well, you could say I have a lot of goals," she began. "First, I would like to put out an album. Maybe I'll tour in the beginning while my recording career is taking off. I plan on singing pop with a little bit of alternative influence. And then once I've made a name for myself I'd like to start a line of clothing. Maybe it could be sold in discount stores because I'd like everyone to be able to afford it. I also plan to start my own magazine—on fashion and music. I'll probably write a few books. Oh, I almost forgot—I'll definitely host my own talk show."

Anna's ideas might sound pretty unrealistic to you, or at least unrealistic for anyone but Oprah. But several years later, she's well on her way, having spent the last two years on a nationwide tour with a band.

When you read Anna's words she sounds ultra-confident. But she wasn't. She was idealistic. She was still aware of the fact that she was a mess. She knew she failed sometimes and hurt people sometimes and didn't do things perfectly most of the time. But she had lots of ideas about what she wanted and believed she could do.

You might not be as idealistic as Anna, but we hope there are a few areas of your life where you feel confident—school, sports, art, chess, theater, music, being a great friend, working with children or the elderly. That confidence is what leads to the kind of idealism Anna had.

Idealism is the belief that you can do anything you put your mind to. Of course, achieving your goals takes hard work, persistence, patience, and willingness to fail now and then. But no one gets what she wants out of life without a little bit of idealism. It's what helps us dream big, what allows us to see the best in ourselves, what pushes us to keep going when we feel like giving up. Oprah wouldn't be Oprah if she didn't believe she could accomplish everything she's set out to do. The same is true for you. You are going to change the world—or at least your corner of it—in ways no one else can.

In truth, it doesn't matter what school you choose, what sorority you pick, or what job you pursue. What matters is that you're true to who you are and who you believe God is creating you to be. Leave the rest up to him.

Purpose

There are a lot of girls who come to Daystar when they are in sixth or seventh grade. After working through whatever they're struggling with, they start helping with our groups and camps for younger kids. And they stick around—for years. We'd like to believe it's because they like us so much.

But the real reason these girls—especially the 17-to-19-year-olds—stick around is because of their sense of purpose. As they work with the younger girls, they see they can make a difference in the lives of other people. And that's an incredible feeling.

One of these girls came to Daystar because she was struggling with bulimia. She fought it long and hard, but she came through it with lots of courage. The next spring we asked her to help with our summer camp for younger kids.

At the end of the camp, she talked to the staff about how grateful she was for the experience. "I don't think I ever believed God could use all of this mess I've been through to help someone else. I'm so happy and feel so much closer to God than I ever have before."

Your life can make a difference. No matter what you've done or been through, God can use you. In fact, it's often the very struggles you've been through that God uses. Put yourself in places where God can use you to touch other people's lives. Go on mission trips. Help with a Habitat for Humanity house. Volunteer with underprivileged kids. Find a way to offer yourself and your gifts to others, and you will be amazed at the sense of purpose you discover.

When I (Sissy) was in high school, one of my best friends had a brilliant idea. She decided that our group of friends should take all of the money we usually spent on Christmas gifts for each other and use it for something else. So we decided to sponsor a family for Christmas. We pooled our money and went shopping. We bought clothes, coats, groceries, toys, and enough food for them to have a huge Christmas dinner. We took it over to the family's house several days before Christmas. I will never forget that day. The mother of the family stood at the door with tears in her eyes, laughing with gratitude at all of our packages.

It took us a total of two afternoons after school—hardly any time or effort. But it was the first time I saw that I could make a difference. We did it every year of high school from then on—as much for ourselves and how good it made us feel as for the families.

So give. Give from your heart and from the gifts God has given you. You are at an age where you not only want to make a difference in the world, but you can. Do it—however and wherever. You will bless others. And you will feel pretty great about yourself in the process.

Independence

Every girl we asked about the best parts of this age talked about independence. You have so much more than ever before—to go out and spend time with your friends, to date, to drive, to stay up later. This independence really hits when you go off to college or move out on your own. Independence is a fantastic high point of these years.

Well, mostly. The quote at the beginning of the last chapter talked about how the writer was more or less able to survive more or less on his own. The *more* and the *less* are a perfect description of these years. Some days you will want all the independence you can have—and even more. Other days you'll want to crawl up in your dad's lap or have your mom take care of you when you get your wisdom teeth out. You want independence where and when you want it, which can be a little confusing for everyone else—it's a little of that ambivalence we talked about earlier.

Still, you are much more independent at this age than you've ever been. You will soon be even more independent. Treat this independence with care. Act in a way that shows you've earned it and can be trusted to handle it. Don't react to the rules of your parents just because they aren't with you every day. Be the person you know God is creating you to be. Give. Trust. Care about others. Make a difference. Be the kind of young woman you imagined you would be one day. There's a wonderful passage in the Bible that we think says a lot about you and all that God is doing in you during these years. James 1:2-4 says, "Consider it a sheer gift, friends, when tests and challenges come at you from all sides. You know that under pressure, your faith-life is forced into the open and shows its true colors. So don't try to get out of anything prematurely. Let it do its work so you can become mature and well-developed, not deficient in any way" (*The Message*).

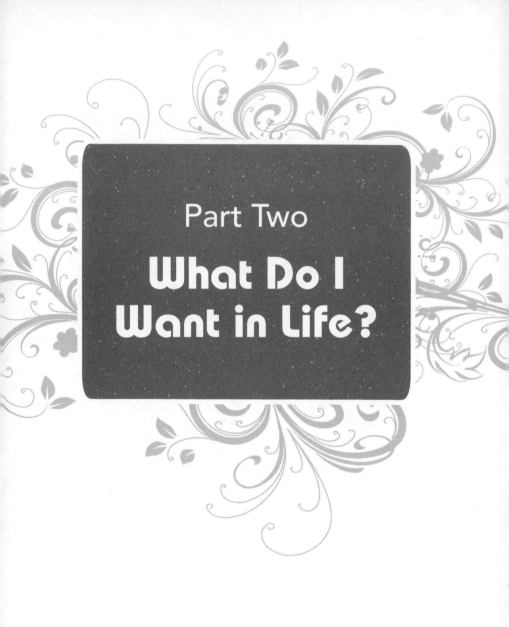

Part Two

What Do I Want in Life?

Chapter 10
With the Heart

It is only with the heart that one can see rightly;
what is essential is invisible to the eye.
— Antoine de Saint-Exupery, The Little Prince

Have you ever noticed that boys don't talk about their hearts very much? But we girls sure do. We have all kinds of terms for what happens to our hearts: Heartache, heartbreak, achy-breaky (just kidding), heavy on our hearts, giving our hearts, protecting our hearts. We spend a lot of time thinking and talking about these hearts of ours.

Physically speaking, our hearts have a vital role to play in keeping us alive. But they have nothing to do with our emotions. It's really our brains that dictate how we feel. Still, the heart symbolizes something that—for females—is as vital in our lives as our actual hearts—relationships.

The importance of relationships
We asked a group of 7-to-19-year-olds what they thought was the hardest part about being a girl. These are their answers:

7-to-9-year-olds
- Other people laughing at me
- Picking clothes out
- Being teased by boys

- Being left out
- Parents yelling at me

10-to-11-year-olds
- Crying
- Shaving, dealing with periods, doing hair
- Being bullied and yelled at in school
- Trying not to gossip
- Keeping up with homework

12-to-14-year-olds
- Dealing with gossip and critical girls
- Having to get the right kind of clothes
- Having to be someone you're not to fit in
- Worrying about peer pressure and what other people think about you
- Worrying about impressing guys
- Dealing with emotions (especially at that time of the month)

15-to-16-year-olds
- Trying to fit in
- Worrying about how you look
- Getting caught in the middle of drama with other girls, fights, competition, overanalyzing things, gossip
- Not knowing if you can trust a guy
- Dealing with periods and maturing faster or slower than your friends

17-to-19-year-olds
- Feeling like you have to look good because you're a girl
- Dealing with how cruel girls are to each other

- Dealing with popularity (or lack of it) and self-esteem (or lack of it)
- Thinking boys will make us happy and then seeing how immature they are at our age
- Dealing with emotions, especially before your period

What do you notice about their answers? The one common factor—across every age group—is relationships. The relationships can be with boys, friends, or parents. Regardless, they are the hardest part for the girls we talked to. What about for you? We would guess that the worst days for you are those when you're fighting with your parents, or breaking up with a guy, or finding out a friend is mad at you. They sure are for us. As one of our friends said, "Relationships are the best and the worst things that happen to us." They cause us stress. They make us worry. They are a part of our lives that determines not only what we think about, but much of who we are.

A few years ago, a country singer named Jessica Andrews had a hit song called "Who I Am" in which she described herself by her relationships—with her grandmother, with her dad, with her mom, with her friends. She ends the chorus by saying, "It's all part of me and that's who I am."

If a guy were singing a song called "Who I Am," it would be about what he does. He might sing, "I'm the football quarterback. I'm good at math. I sing and play the guitar." (Okay, maybe he'd say it better than that, but you get the idea). Somewhere in there he might say, "I'm Susan's boyfriend" or "I'm Matt's best friend." The relationships would be in there, but they wouldn't be the primary way a guy would define himself.

The female heart
Psychologists have spent a lot of time trying to describe the dif-

ferences between men and women. They use words such as *independence* and *interdependence*, *purpose* and *intimacy*, *significance* and *security*. You know enough about boys by now to guess who wants more of what.

The labels used for the differences between the ways guys and girls think about relationships might be new, but the differences themselves aren't. The Gospel of John describes the dissimilarity between men and women in a surprising way.

Here's the story up to this point: Jesus has been crucified. The disciples are grieving. It is now Sunday, and Mary Magdalene is going to check on Jesus' tomb. When she gets there, she realizes the stone covering the tomb has been rolled away. You can imagine how she feels. This man she followed, who meant the world to her, was brutally killed. Now his body has disappeared. She is freaked out and goes to find her friends, hoping they'll know what to do.

Mary finds Peter and John and tells them what's going on. As you read what happens next, notice the differences in the way the men and women deal with this shocking turn of events:

So Peter and the other disciple started for the tomb. Both were running, but the other disciple outran Peter and reached the tomb first. He bent over and looked in at the strips of linen lying there but did not go in. Then Simon Peter came along behind him and went straight into the tomb. He saw the strips of linen lying there, as well as the cloth that had been around Jesus' head. The cloth was still lying in its place, separate from the linen. Finally the other disciple, who had reached the tomb first, also went inside. He saw and believed. (They still did not understand from Scripture that Jesus had to rise from the dead.) Then the disciples went back to where they were staying.

Now Mary stood outside the tomb crying. As she wept, she bent over to look into the tomb and saw two angels in white, seat-ed where Jesus' body had been, one at the head and the other at the foot. They asked her, "Woman, why are you crying?"

"They have taken my Lord away," she said, "and I don't know where they have put him." At this, she turned around and saw Jesus standing there, but she did not realize that it was Jesus.

He asked her, "Woman, why are you crying? Who is it you are looking for?" Thinking he was the gardener, she said, "Sir, if you have carried him away, tell me where you have put him, and I will get him."

Jesus said to her, "Mary." She turned toward him and cried out in Aramaic, "Rabboni!" (which means "Teacher"). (John 20:3-16)

Did you see some differences? Let's look at how the guys reacted to the news that Jesus' body was gone:

1) They raced to the tomb. "Both were running, but the other disciple outran Peter and reached the tomb first." Obviously, John won and he wants us to know it. He even says it twice.

2) They got there and realized that the clothes Jesus had been wearing were lying there in an organized way. If someone had stolen Jesus' body, they probably wouldn't have taken the time to leave everything nice and neat. So the guys reasoned that Jesus was gone of his own will—he had risen from the dead.

But where was Mary? She was outside the tomb weeping. Mary was upset. She was worried about the body of her friend. Yes, he was dead, but her care and concern for him were not. The guys got their competition over with, realized Jesus had risen, and left. And Mary was still crying.

Two angels showed up to ask Mary what was wrong. She said—through lots of tears—"They have taken my Lord away." Then Jesus appeared. Mary saw Jesus but was too emotional to recognize him. It was only when Jesus called Mary by name that she realized who he was.

Isn't that just like a girl? One of our relationships hits a huge bump and our emotions take over. Our hearts not only pump blood, they pump plenty of drama, too. So much so that we often don't recognize the ways God steps into the middle of our pain. We miss God's comfort or his words to us because we are focused on our own hurt.

We are hung up on relationships. And they truly are the best and worst part of being a girl. We know—or at least want to know—what it's like to have deep, meaningful friendships. We know how to give of ourselves and share our hearts with others. And we know how to treasure our friends through good times and bad. Just think, if it hadn't been for Mary heading out to check on Jesus that Sunday morning, who knows when the guys would have discovered that the first life-changing Easter had actually begun.

Chapter 11
Relentless Reminders

Our longings for relationships are relentless reminders of what we were made for and what is worth living for.
— *Sharon A. Hersh,* Bravehearts

As girls, we are wired for relationships. Think back to the chapters on development at the beginning of this book: Oxytocin, awareness, responsiveness, acceptance—all of these lead up to the fact that relationships are truly essential for girls. We long for them. We see who we are against the backdrop of the people with whom we are in relationships.

We would guess that when you look back over the happiest times of your life, most of them involve some type of relationship. We would guess the saddest times do, too. Relationships have a great deal of power over us. They remind us—often relentlessly—of how God designed us.

The people who come to Daystar are a good example of this truth. A lot of the boys in counseling are there to help them stop fighting with their friends or figure out why they are struggling in school or deal with something hard that's happening in their families. And we have some young girls in counseling for the same reasons. But while we have one group for second-through-fourth-grade girls, we have five groups for high school girls. Something happens to girls when they become teenagers that can send them down a path of worry, fear, and anxiety. And that's when they come to us.

We know exactly what that "something" is: Relationships. When girls move into adolescence, they start to worry. Does she want to be my friend? Does he like me? Are my parents mad at me? How can I be myself and still be accepted? Why would a boy like me? These and a million other questions bounce around girls' heads every day. As one girl told us, "There is so much going on in a girl's head that it's easy to let other people think for you."

That would be great if those "other people" always made good decisions and loved everyone perfectly. But they don't— and neither do you. The hard part of relationships is that other people inevitably disappoint you. They don't act the way you want them to, they don't say what you think they should, they hurt you, they fail you, they forget you. The rude awakening of being a teenager is that the disappointment doesn't end just because you and the people you care about are a little older and more mature. The fact is people hurt each other no matter how old they are.

Several years ago, I (Melissa) was meeting with a high school girl and her mom. As I sat with them this girl spilled out a list of things she wanted to be different in her relationship with her mom. At the end of the list she said very loudly, "I just want to be loved correctly!"

We all want that same thing. We want to be loved all the time and never disappointed. We want to feel safe and connected and close and important to someone else. We want to be loved correctly. But we're not—at least not by other people.

Your hurting heart

Let's say you've got a cut on your leg. You have several options:

1) You could ignore it. This is actually what Melissa does

most of the time. Every day of camp she has blood trickling down her leg from something. One of the kids will point to her leg and Melissa will say, "What? Oh, that's nothing."

2) You can try to distract yourself. This is what mothers do when their toddlers get a little bit hurt. We know a one-year-old named Afton. One afternoon we were all outside and Afton fell down, hurt his head, and started screaming. So we checked him out, saw that he was okay, and gave him ice cream. We thought if he could get his mind off the pain and do something that made him feel better he would forget to feel bad.

3) You can get mad at yourself for being hurt. Several years ago, there was a video circulating of a professional gymnast. He was doing the pommel horse at a competition. He chalked his hands, stood back in position, and made a serious run for the horse. When he got up to it to throw his body onto it, he did just that. His hands missed it entirely. Rather than swinging over the horse he landed on it, chest first. The blow must have hurt. But his physical pain was nothing compared to how angry he was at himself for falling. As this athlete walked back to the starting line for another try, he picked up a folding chair and broke it over his head. His response might not make sense to us, but it did to him.

We tend to deal with the pain in our hearts in similar ways.

1) Ignoring it

In 12-step groups this is called denial. We see a lot of girls in our offices whose favorite sentence is, "I'm used to it." One girl said to us, "I'd rather not feel at all than feel disappointed." These girls hope that by acting like they're not hurt, they will stop hurting.

In spite of their words the pain in these girls' lives is obvious—their actions speak a whole lot louder than their words.

When the parents of these girls come in, they tell us about their daughters' anger, their rage. The girls yell at their siblings. They yell at their parents. They get mad about the tiniest problems. The feelings they want to pretend don't exist are spilling out all over their families.

Your feelings will always come out somewhere. If someone at school hurts your feelings and you don't ever talk about it, you will find yourself getting angry—angrier than the situation calls for—with your other friends or your family. Feelings need an outlet, and if you don't give them a healthy one, they'll find an unhealthy one instead. And that's where this next attempt at dealing with your pain comes in.

2) Distracting yourself

When people are trying to get over an addiction, they often replace that addiction with another one. So someone might stop smoking and start eating too much. Someone else might stop cutting herself and start drinking.

Of course these replacement addictions aren't always obvious addictions. Remember little Afton who fell down and got hurt? We used ice cream to distract him from his pain. For girls your age, that distraction can still be ice cream—or it can be no food at all. It can be alcohol, television, drugs, cutting, shopping, even exercise. Anything you do to distract yourself from the pain you feel inside can become an addiction.

The problem is that these addictions do distract you— at least, temporarily. When you're drunk you don't feel pain. When you buy your eighth pair of trendy jeans for the week, you feel better. But the pain that led you to these distractions hasn't gone away. It will keep popping up, and you'll keep trying to push it back down. The longer you try to distract yourself, the more powerful that pain will become and the more distractions you will need to keep it from taking over.

It's a terrible cycle and it almost always ends in far more pain than whatever you were trying to cover up to begin with.

If you feel like you're doing something to distract yourself from pain—even if it's something that seems harmless, like shoe shopping or running—please talk to someone. Talk to your parents, to an adult you trust, to your school counselor. The sooner you deal with the pain that's leading you to the behavior, the sooner you'll be free from the even more significant pain that the behaviors cause.

3) Blaming yourself

We girls are great at this one. We're like that gymnast who hit himself over the head with a chair because he made an embarrassing—and painful!—mistake. We even take it a step further.

I (Sissy) remember talking to a 17-year-old whose boyfriend of two years had just broken up with her. Her response was, "Why am I so stupid?" She wasn't stupid. Her intelligence had nothing to do with the fact that he hurt her.

Her response was tragically typical for a lot of girls (and women). We get our feelings hurt and think we did something wrong—I shouldn't have trusted that person. I shouldn't have put myself in that situation. On and on, until we make ourselves feel even worse than we did when we got hurt.

And that's why we do it. When we blame ourselves, we are in control of our own pain. It seems easier that way because we don't have to accept that someone else's actions can change the way we feel. We think we'll feel less manipulated, less vulnerable, less fooled by people we trusted. And we can also still think the best of them. We can still believe they like us or care about us and that things fell apart because of our failure. It's sometimes easier to believe you did something wrong rather than believe someone just doesn't want to be your friend.

Each of these three tactics is about control. They are our attempts to make our hearts less open to pain. But that's never going to happen—not without you shutting down all the good parts of yourself, too. When we close our hearts to pain, we also close them to joy, to love, to happiness. And that goes against everything we were created for.

We long for relationships, to be close and connected to other people. Yet every relationship will bring a little pain with it. That's what sin does to relationships.

We were created to live in perfect connection to God and to other people. But when sin came into the world through Adam and Eve, we started to lose those perfect relationships. They became tainted by selfishness and shame. So we don't work perfectly, we don't live perfectly, and we certainly don't love perfectly. People disappoint us. And if we're honest with ourselves, we know we do our share of disappointing, too.

There are ways to respond to all this disappointment and pain that can help you instead of adding to your hurt. They aren't easy to learn, but they can help you live your life with an open heart.

Healing your heart

Take another look at that quote at the beginning of the last chapter. It says, "It is only with the heart that one can see rightly." That's a pretty profound statement. Love helps us see the good in people, to see them the way God sees them—as unique creations who are worthy of great love.

Ignoring our hearts, seeking distractions, and blaming ourselves keep us from seeing "rightly." We only see how we've been hurt. And even though those efforts to avoid dealing with our pain don't work, we keep using them. We use more drugs. We blame ourselves with such conviction that we start to hurt ourselves. We lose the ability to trust other people, to risk real relationships. This is not seeing rightly. It's more like seeing selfishly. It's all about us and how others are, or are not, meeting our needs.

To see rightly is to see a bigger picture. It is to see that you are hurt—and that you hurt others. It is to see that even though your parents make mistakes, they aren't out to get you. It is to see that your friends aren't trying to hurt you but that they're doing their best to navigate life—just like you. When you focus on how the people you love have failed you, you can only see how the people you love have failed you.

We're not saying you should ignore the hurt. We're saying you will feel it—and you will dish it out yourself from time to time. When you're hurt, talk to someone you trust. Write in a journal. Paint. Play a musical instrument. Find outlets for your emotions that are productive rather than destructive. You are created for relationships—and that means you will experience all the highs and lows that come with them. Let those feelings out—the good ones and the not-so-good ones. When you work through those feelings with a friend or through art or music or writing, you'll discover the kind of truth about yourself that is often found only in hard times.

You will be disappointed. You will be hurt and even betrayed at times. But like Mary, we girls run the risk of being stuck at the tomb, so caught up in our pain that we miss Jesus standing right beside us. With God's help we can deal with our hurt in healthy, productive ways. We can repair damaged friendships, work though family struggles. We can keep our hearts open to the goodness of other people and experience the joy and beauty of deep, meaningful relationships.

In Luke's Gospel, Jesus visits the home of two sisters, Mary and Martha. The women love Jesus and consider him their friend. They want to connect with him. So Martha gets busy. She cleans and prepares and cooks. You could even say she ignores and distracts. Mary, on the other hand, does something different. She sits down with Jesus and talks to him. She listens to him. She gives him her time and attention. Then Jesus says, "Martha, Martha,...you are worried and upset about many things, but few things are needed—or indeed only one. Mary has chosen what is better, and it will not be taken away from her" (Luke 10:41-42).

While Martha keeps busy, Mary sits at the feet of Jesus. In fact this Mary, who is called Mary of Bethany, is sitting at Jesus' feet each time she is mentioned in the Bible. Time after time, she chooses what is needed.

Relationships are central to who we are as girls. But only one relationship will never disappoint you, and that's the one you have with God. God, who knows you and loves you and cares for you more than any person ever could, has promised never to leave us. The Bible says, "The Lord himself goes before you and will be with you; he will never leave you nor forsake you. Do not be afraid; do not be discouraged" (Deuteronomy 31:8). God will be with you through all your disappointments, all your pain, and all your relationships. Even when friends fail you, there is one friend who never will. And he knows your heart better than anyone.

Chapter 12
The Relationship Chapter: Girls

Loneliness was easy. Any fool could put out his tongue at his fellow man and turn his back, but worthwhile union was, he could see, hard work. — Elizabeth Goudge, Island Magic

We don't want to think of relationships as hard work. We want friendships without conflict. We want romance without disappointment. We want to live the fairy tale. But we have bad news for you: There is no fairy tale. (That's actually pretty good news but it doesn't sound like it at first.) Sure, it might feel like you've found Prince Charming when you're on the first date or even during the first month of a new relationship. But if you have had a close friend or boyfriend for any length of time, you know the truth. Relationships are hard work.

Here's why that's good news. The work that goes into relationships is what connects our hearts to each other and to God in deeper and more intimate ways than we can imagine. Real life—even with all its messiness and pain and disappointment—is much better than any fairy tale.

Did you read any of the *Series of Unfortunate Events* books when you were younger? Lemony Snicket says, "Friends can make you feel that the world is smaller and less sneaky than it really is." When our friendships are at their best, that's exactly how they make us feel—connected, safe. But then your friend starts dating the guy who just broke up with you. Or your best friend invites someone else to go to the beach with her family over spring break.

When these kinds of situations come up, that Lemony Snicket quote works in reverse. Rather than friends making you feel like the world is smaller and less sneaky, you feel smaller and they seem sneaky. We know because we've been there ourselves. And we've talked to a lot of girls who also feel small and sneaked up on sometimes. We thought you might like to hear what other girls like you are dealing with in their friendships. You might find that your friendship struggles are a lot like the ones these girls are facing. We'll also show you how we responded to these situations, to give you some ideas on how you can tackle some of the toughest friendship challenges.

Dear Melissa and Sissy,

I'm really worried about my friend. We've been best friends since we were little. We've gone to church together forever. We had promised each other we would never do the bad stuff in high school like drinking and drugs. But she does now. She tries to do it without me finding out. What do I do? How can I help her and not make her feel like I'm being judgmental? — Caroline, 17

Caroline,

It can be really hard to watch this happen with a friend. Just the fact that you are writing and worried about her says a lot about how much you care.

First, pray for her. God can do much more through his Spirit than you could ever do through your words. Then, if you feel like he's leading you to, talk to her. But as you do, remember that we all mess up. And God doesn't say that one mess is bigger than the other. If you speak to her from the perspective of someone who is also a mess, she won't feel judged. If you come to her like she is the problem and you're going to solve it, she probably will. Say what you can and then just continue to be who you are. She may not respond right away; she may not for months or even years. The outcome is not up to you. But you can be a reminder to her of God's grace and love—through your actions, your words, and your heart for her. And keep praying!

If you're like Caroline's friend—or if you've ever been confronted by someone like Caroline—know these friends are talking to you because they care about you. They might not have done it perfectly, they might have been a little judgmental, but they were still trying to do what they thought was best for you. Proverbs 27:6 says, "Faithful are the wounds of a friend, but deceitful are the kisses of an enemy" (NASB). Listen to the words of your friends even if their delivery isn't perfect. Your friends deserve your trust far more than the people around you who tell you whatever you want to hear. True friends care enough about you to tell you the hard truth. Once you hear it, it's up to you to do what's right and be true to who God has called you to be.

Dear Melissa and Sissy,

I have a really fun group of friends at my school. I love hanging out with them. We have a lot in common. Some of us even go to the same church. But it just seems like our relationships are shallow. I'm afraid to talk to them about things that bother me because they don't talk about that kind of stuff. What do I do? How do I go deeper with people? How do I talk to them about God and our lives, rather than just what we're doing on Friday night? — Emily, 16

Emily,

We're so glad to hear that you want deeper relationships with your friends. High school friendships can be difficult because you're all maturing at different speeds. So you can have deeper connections with some people, but end up with shallow friendships with

others. The tricky part is figuring out which friendships are which. You could start by revealing a little more about yourself. Talk about how you feel when something is hard for you or tell your friend something you have been learning about God. See how she responds. If that friend wants a deeper relationship too, she'll probably show a real interest in what you're saying. She might even tell you something similar. If she doesn't say much, or if she changes the subject, she might be happy with the way things are for now. It can take a little while to find those friends you can share your heart with—but it's well worth the effort!

It can be scary to talk about deeper feelings and ideas. It used to terrify me (Sissy) to talk about myself. But relationships are much richer when you're willing to share your true self—flaws, doubts, struggles, and all—with someone. It's a rare and precious gift to find a friend who will support, encourage, challenge, laugh, love, and pursue Christ with you. To have this kind of friend, you have to be willing to go there yourself.

Sissy and Melissa,

One of my best friends does the same thing every time she gets a new boyfriend. When she's in between guys or even has a crush on a new guy, we talk a lot. She goes out with our group of friends on the weekends, calls, texts, and all of that. Then when she starts dating someone, she disappears. None of us see or even hear from her. I feel like we're great friends when she's not dating anyone and don't know each other when she is. I've tried to talk to her, but things just don't seem to change. What can I do? — Claire, 15

Claire,

We talk to a lot of girls in your situation—and hers. On one hand, you understand that she's excited to have a boyfriend. On the other hand you miss talking and hanging out with her. Some

girls just seem to have a harder time dating and staying connected to their friends at the same time.

One of the hardest parts of growing up is letting your friends make their own choices. You can talk to her but to continue to talk to her about it is probably just going to push her toward whoever she's dating. Tell her how you feel, then enjoy your other friends. She might feel like she's missing out, she might not. But you want her to hang out with you because she wants to be with you, not because she feels guilted into it.

If you're like Claire's friend, it might be hard to understand why your friends are disappointed when you don't spend as much time with them as you used to. Well, they're disappointed because they care. It can be so fun to have a boyfriend, but hang on to your girl friends, too. The truth is, you'll either marry your boyfriend or you won't. If you do, you've got the rest of your life to be with him. If you don't, it would be a bummer to have missed out on time with your friends for some guy who's only in the picture for a few months.

When you start dating, it can be tempting to put everything else in your life on hold and spend all your time and energy on your boyfriend. We strongly suggest you not do that. As fun as it can be, dating is not the only important part of your life right now. Your memories of high school will be full of friends, family, athletics, arts, school, and all kinds of wonderful experiences. You've got so much to discover and learn about who you are and all God has in store for you. If you pour all of your time into one guy (or even just one friend), you'll miss out on so many other good, fun moments.

Sissy and Melissa,

There is a girl at my school who is really sweet—and really clingy. She follows my group of friends around. She asks us what she should wear, what she should do about all kinds of different things, and even what she should eat for meals. I don't want to be mean to her, but I'm not sure what to do. Sometimes my friends and I want to have time with just us. What should we do? — Jessie, 17

Jessie,

It is really hard to know what to do in this situation—and almost every one of us can relate. It's obviously a compliment to you and your friends that this girl wants to hang out with you, but it sounds like she'd like more attention from you. You don't want to hurt her but you want a little space.

You can tell her this in a kind way. Think about how you would want someone to talk to you if you were in her shoes. You can say something like, "I really would like to be your friend. But part of being a friend is giving each other space to do your own thing and have other friends, too. When you ask my advice all the time, it pushes me away." You may even have to say it a few times before she really understands. Some people have a harder time than others understanding the rhythms of relationships. Be patient with her, and please continue to be kind. You never know when you might end up being the slightly annoying friend in her shoes!

Sometimes friends pull away and you don't understand why. It's often because of situations like the one Jessie described. Maybe your friends feel like they need a little more space. Maybe you've tried to be more like your friends, hoping to fit in instead of being yourself.

Whatever the reason, it's good to remember: Friendships do have a rhythm. There's a balance between spending time together and giving each other space. It helps each person feel like she is her own person within the friendship (and as we said earlier, the same balance is important in guy/girl relationships).

Confidence helps too. Girls have a hard time hanging out with other girls who seem insecure—which is ironic because we all are. Maybe that's why we're drawn to girls who seem confident. But even if you don't feel so confident, you can act like you are. Figure out how you want to dress and what you like to do and read and watch and play. Hang out with different groups of people. Most of all, reach out to other people, not just one person or one group. There are a whole lot of other people out there who will feel lucky to be your friend.

Dear Melissa and Sissy,

I have been in the same group of friends since junior high—and they sometimes act like they're still in junior high. They get mad at each other and talk behind each other's backs. I don't know what to do. How do I stop them from backstabbing and gossiping about each other? And how can I be in a group that is considered popular and still be kind to other people? I don't want to get lost in all of the gossip and girl drama that goes on. — Allie, 15

Dear Allie,

It's funny how everyone sets their sights on being part of the popular group. But once you get there, it's not really all it's cracked up to be. The popular people often are the ones who talk behind each other's backs the most because they feel they need to protect their status.

When your friends start gossiping, walk away. Or, you could defend the person being talked about. Or, you could even say something like, "I sure hope we have better things to talk about than the people who are supposed to be our best friends." They may get mad at you at first—but only because they know you're right.

As far as being kind to other people, just be kind. It really is that simple. Be yourself and who you know God has called you to be. Don't worry about your friends getting jealous because you're hanging out with other people. We all get jealous and insecure from time to time. If they're really your friends, they'll like you no matter who your other friends are. If they continue to be mad, you can talk to them about it. But you might not need friends who get mad at you for caring about other people.

Gossip can be a huge problem in friendships. It's so easy to get hooked into talking about other people. But nothing good comes of gossip—that's why the Bible tells us to avoid it whenever we can. (There are six verses warning against gossip in the book of Proverbs alone!) Gossip can make you feel powerful, but it only makes you look insecure.

Most of the time gossip is a way of dealing with feelings of jealousy. Girls tend to gossip about people they think are better than them in some way. We hope that whoever hears the gossip will think less of the person we've been talking about. But again, often the only person who looks bad is the person doing the gossiping.

You don't want to be known as the person who gossips or the friend who's jealous or even as the mean, intimidating girl of the group. If you're struggling with gossip or jealousy, ask God to help you stop. Pray for your heart to soften toward others so you can see them the way God sees them. Ask God to give you confidence, mixed with humility and kindness, mixed with awareness of your friends. You'll end up feeling better about them—and yourself.

Being a good friend
Some girls have an easy time making and keeping friends. Naturally they have low points and disappointments like everyone else, but they seem to have fewer of them. Friendships just seem to come naturally for them. But other girls struggle with friendships almost constantly. If you're one of those girls, you know it's not always easy to strike up a friendship or maintain a connection in the midst of all the changes that go on in these years.

We asked some of the girls we know to share their advice on making and keeping friends. We're hoping it might be just what you need to hear.

- Don't flirt with someone one of your friends likes. It's backstabbing your friend. If you like the guy, talk to your friend about it. You are friends with your friends for the rest of your life. It's not worth losing a friendship over a guy you might date for a few weeks.
- Don't tell your friends' secrets. Be trustworthy and keep your promises. And don't gossip. There are other things that are much more fun.
- Don't create drama for the sake of drama. If you're always in some kind of crisis, you probably need to talk to a school counselor. If you're making up a crisis to get attention, your friends are going to get tired of it.
- Don't worry about what other people think. You want to respect other people's opinions, but you don't have to morph into who they think you should be. Be yourself or you're not going to be happy.

When asked the greatest commandment of all, Jesus' response was, "Love the Lord your God with all your heart and with all your soul and with all your mind." The second most important was this: "Love your neighbor as yourself" (see Matthew 22:36-40). Loving other people ranks pretty high up there on the list. And that doesn't just mean loving the people you like. It also means loving the mean girls and the annoying ones. It means loving the people who hurt you, who disappoint you.

Relationships are hard work. But they are still one of the best parts of life as a girl, and they are well worth every bit of the effort.

Chapter 13
The Relationship Chapter: Guys

If you, my dear father, will not take the trouble of checking her exuberant spirits, and of teaching her that her present pursuits are not to be the business of her life, she will soon be beyond the reach of amendment. Her character will be fixed, and she will, at sixteen, be the most determined flirt that ever made herself and her family ridiculous.
— *Jane Austen*, Pride and Prejudice

Whether they're just friends or boyfriends, guys are a bigger part of your life now than they have been before. But these relationships take work, too. And they don't take the type of work that Jane Austen is talking about. It's a different kind of work than your friendships with girls because, obviously, boys are different. And they can be a real mystery.

Developing relationships with boys comes with a whole new set of expectations and understandings. So we decided to talk to a group of guys your age. We asked them a bunch of questions from girls your age. These are their insightful—albeit very short—answers in their own words (difference #1—guys talk a lot less than girls!).

What do guys think about?
Cars, sports, sports, and more sports, ESPN, the future, girls, movies, food, music, MySpace, and Facebook.

What do guys look for in a girlfriend?
Personality, looks (they don't have to look perfect, just decent), similar interests, values, modest dress, someone who doesn't ask trick questions, and someone who doesn't talk too much.

What are some of your pet peeves about girls?
They put themselves down, compare themselves to other girls, sulk, act bossy or controlling, dress a certain way to get attention, people pleasing, when they say, "Call me" and then act too busy to talk to you, saying, "Can you leave us alone for a minute?"

What should a girl do if she likes a guy?
Make eye contact and be yourself. Don't act stuck up or condescending.

How do you like girls to dress?
Modestly, in whatever you feel comfortable, not in all black, not in things like mini-skirts that are really revealing.

Does the way girls dress really affect guys?
Yes! It's distracting to us when we're trying to think about you as a person.

How important is it to you not to have sex before marriage?
On a scale of one to ten, it's an eleven—really important. And if a guy doesn't feel the same way, date a different guy.

Why do guys say things that are gross or perverted sometimes?
It's funny to us. We have a different sense of humor. We like gross—but not perverted.

What do guys talk about when there aren't any girls around?
Food, sports, girls—we don't really talk a lot.

Why do guys exaggerate physical stuff in relationships?
To feel powerful, to impress other people—only it usually doesn't.

Why do guys try to annoy and tease girls?
It's our way of relating to you. We goof off when we feel comfortable—or uncomfortable.

Why do guys have a hard time being just friends?
Because spending time together, talking, and touching as friends can lead to other emotions, and we'll assume there's something between us when there isn't.

Why do guys get jealous when we talk to other guys?
Because we feel like they're competition. We get jealous and want all the attention. We can be a little insecure.

Do you think it's better to be friends before you date a girl?
Yes!

How do I help my guy friends talk about their feelings?
We need to trust you and feel like you're honest. Reassure us our conversation is confidential. You might have to push us a little.

Why do guys have a hard time staying friends after a break-up?
It's awkward. Give us a little time and then approach us.

What do you think are good physical boundaries in a relationship?
First, you need to talk about it on the front end and compare

your values. Don't have sex. Never be in the same bed, even if you're just watching TV. And keep your hands off anything covered by any type of underwear.

How's that for honesty? Were you surprised by any of their answers? Yes, guys are different, but they aren't always as different as we girls think they are. They are sensitive, they feel insecure, they want to be liked and appreciated and treated with respect. True, they don't talk much and when they do, the chances are good it will be about sports. But they are doing their best to make relationships work, just like we are.

The girls at Daystar wanted the boys to ask them questions back. We thought you would enjoy reading their questions. These give you an even better idea of what they think about—and what they think you think about.

Why do girls not tell you everything up front?

What do girls look for in guys?

Does it matter to you what we wear?

Why do you dress in a revealing way if you know it might lead guys on and give them ideas if you don't want them to have those ideas?

Why do you go to the bathroom together and what do you talk about in there?

What do you enjoy doing on dates?

What pet peeves do you have about guys?

How far in the future are you thinking when you date a guy?

Why do you get jealous when we talk to other girls?

Do girls kiss because they enjoy it or just because they think it pleases the guy?

What's the sweetest thing a guy can do for a girl?

Why do you insist on asking us if we like certain celebrities?

Why don't you believe us when we tell you that you're beautiful?

You are valuable. You deserve to be in relationships with friends and boys who see you that way. But you have to do your part to make that happen. You need to expect to be treated that way—even when you don't feel it. Friends will value you more if you value yourself. Guys will respect you more if you respect yourself. Think about what this means for you— for your relationships with friends and for your relationships with guys. We believe it starts with simply being yourself.

Relationships are hard because we disappoint each other. Don't look to one relationship to be the fulfillment of all that is lacking in your life. No boyfriend is ever going to be that. But Jesus is. He is the friend who sticks closer than a brother (Proverbs 18:24). He will never let you down, never gossip about you, always has your very best interests at heart. And he wants to give you relationships that reflect his heart for you. Watch for them. Enjoy them. And allow him to use you in other people's lives to do that same kind of reflecting.

Chapter 14
Returning Thanks

The choice for gratitude rarely comes without some real effort. But each time I make it, the next choice is a little easier, a little freer, a little less self-conscious. Because every gift I acknowledge reveals another and another.
— *Henri Nouwen,* The Return of the Prodigal Son

On a scale from 1 to 10, how thankful would you say you are for your family? We're not talking about being thankful when they drive you to a friend's house or when they finally give you a present you've been asking for. We're talking about being thankful for being loved and provided for. So how thankful are you? Now here's another very important question: How thankful do *they* think you are?

My (Sissy's) grandfather starts off every Thanksgiving, Christmas, and Easter meal by saying "Please bow your heads so we can return thanks." He's the only person I've ever heard use this phrase "return thanks" when asking people to pray. But it makes so much sense. As a family we are giving God our gratitude for all he has given us. We're returning thanks.

This chapter is about returning thanks to your family. We would guess that, although you feel pretty thankful for your family—at least some of the time—they don't necessarily know it. If you grew up in a Christian family, you learned how to show your gratitude to God through prayer and worship.

But most of us do a pretty lousy job of returning thanks to the people in our lives. It might come a little more naturally with some of them. If one of your friends tells you they're thankful for you, you probably tell them back. But the people in your family are often the very last ones to hear your words of gratitude or know how you feel about them.

At our summer camps we often see significant changes in kids' lives. It might be that they decide to live their lives for Jesus or make a commitment to be a better friend, a more patient daughter, a kinder sister. And they do that—at camp. But several weeks later we see the parents of these very same kids at Daystar.

"What happened at camp?" they ask us. "I know you said it was a great week for Catherine, but she came home as grumpy as ever, if not more. She slept the whole car ride back, and I've hardly seen her since she's been home. She's with her friends constantly. When I try to talk to her, she just gets angry. I thought she matured this summer, but she seems to be moving backward."

We tell these parents that home is often the last place they'll see changes in their children. Why? Because most of us take our families for granted. We know they're not going anywhere, no matter how awful we are to them. We know they'll love us—no matter what. So our families get the brunt of all our bad moods and irritability. You know how it goes: You spend all day at school being kind and patient and friendly to everyone.

By the time you get home you're exhausted. Rather than getting your kindness, your family gets your grumpy leftovers—impatience, frustration, a short temper.

There's another problem with taking your family for granted—a loss of gratitude. How many hours of their lives have your parents spent driving you from one place to another? How many hours have they spent at work trying to earn money to pay for your clothes, or your activities, or your toys, or the gas for all that driving? How many cards have you received from your grandparents? How many times have your siblings shared their stuff with you or helped you with a problem or let you hang out with them, even when you were bugging them?

These questions aren't meant to make you feel guilty. They are meant to inspire gratitude—a sense of thankfulness—in you. We know, as Henri Nouwen said in the quotation at the beginning of this chapter, that gratitude doesn't come without some real effort—especially with our families. For all of us, even those of us beyond the age of 19, our families are often at the back of the line when it comes to showing gratitude.

Recently I (Melissa) met with 17-year-old Maggie and her dad. Maggie's parents are divorced and she lives with her mom during the week and with her dad every other weekend. But as Maggie has gotten older and busier, it's been getting harder and harder for her to get to her dad's on those weekends. She's a cheerleader, so Fridays are booked with football games. Saturday nights she is either with friends or her boyfriend. When it's time to go home, she's too tired to pack a bag and head over to her dad's. Sounds understandable, doesn't it?

Not from her dad's perspective. He sees that in two years Maggie will go off to college. His time with her is running out, and he wants to be with her as much as he can. So he feels very strongly about spending every other weekend with her—no matter what she has planned. He doesn't want her to cancel on her friends. He just wants her at his house so he can at least have breakfast with her on Saturdays and go to church with her on Sundays. He doesn't think it's a lot to ask.

Maggie and her dad are at a stalemate. If you don't play chess, that means neither of them is able or willing to move. She wants the convenience of her mom's house. He wants to be with Maggie.

I told Maggie the same thing we're telling you. Make the effort. Your family may not have been the perfect representation of what a family should be. No family is. But you can still be grateful for them. You can show them by what you say and how you act that you appreciate what they have done for you—no matter how much or how little you think that is.

Your real family
When you were a child you didn't say, "Thank you, Mommy" every time your mom did something nice for you. But you smiled at her. You hugged her. You acted in a way that showed your thankfulness.

Back then, your mom was your hero. Both of your parents were. And even though you got really mad at your siblings now and then, you still loved them and wanted to play with them a minute after the argument ended.

But now the awareness you've developed over the past few years has made it a little more difficult to just forgive and forget. You recognize the ways your parents hurt you. You see how they hurt each other. You notice that your dad doesn't come home as much as you think he should. Maybe he even left your mom and married someone else. You've noticed that the grandmother you used to think was the most loving person ever is actually really critical of your mom. You see your family as they really are.

As this awareness grows, you have a choice to make. One option is to distance yourself from your family. They used to be perfect in your eyes. Now they're not. You can decide that, since they're not perfect, they have nothing to offer you and you don't want them in your life anymore. If you think that sounds extreme, you should know that we talk to teenagers every day who have decided to do just that—get away from their families. Sometimes it's a physical move to another home, like the home of their other parent. Sometimes it's an emotional move—they stop talking, stop relating, stop engaging.

Another option—the better option—is to offer grace and gratitude. Your dad might have left your mom. She might still be angry at him. But he didn't leave because of you. Even if he's not a perfect dad, you can still have a relationship with him. You can enjoy and even appreciate what he does offer.

Maybe you've realized your mom is a perfectionist and can be really critical of you. That doesn't mean you can't still have a meaningful relationship with her. Tell her—kindly—when she hurts your feelings. Tell her you need her encouragement and support. Do your part to stay connected and grateful.

Think about the times you've messed up or hurt your parents or a sibling. What you wanted most in those moments was grace. You want to be accepted and loved in spite of your weaknesses. You can do the same for your family.

We know there are plenty of families where it can be hard to find a reason to be grateful for anything. We have a friend named Lindsey whose father has a severe anger problem. Most of the time things are great between the two of them. They have dinners together, go to plays, and have a lot of fun. But every so often something sets off Lindsey's dad and he explodes. He yells at her and says horrible things to her, things that are hard to forgive, much less forget.

Lindsey has several different options with her dad. She can naively ignore this problem—never talk about how it affects her and pretend it doesn't exist. But as you know, Lindsey's feelings will just come out somewhere else.

Lindsey could also walk away from her dad. She could decide that his anger is too much and cut off her relationship with him entirely. But if Lindsey did that she would miss out on the times when her relationship with her dad is really good.

Fortunately, there is another way. Lindsey can face the reality of her relationship with her father. She can start to respond differently. She may never teach him to handle his anger in an appropriate way, but she can make sure he doesn't handle it inappropriately around her. When he starts to yell at her on the phone, Lindsey can say something like, "Dad, I'm not going to talk to you when you're like this. You'll just say things that will make both of us feel worse later. Why don't you call me back when you're not so angry?" Even if he calls back repeatedly, Lindsey doesn't have to answer the phone.

Maybe the parent you have a hard time with lives with you. In that case, counseling can be a great idea. Talk to your school counselor, or ask your parents to take you to a counselor outside of school. If it feels scary to tell your mom or dad that you want counseling because of your relationship with them, the counselor can help you handle that. Just tell your parents you have some things going on in your life that you'd like some help with. A good counselor can take it from there.

If counseling isn't an option, then try talking to your parents. We know this can be really hard. But if you find a time when both of you are feeling calm and unemotional, tell your mom and dad what you're struggling with. Let them know that you're hurt by what they're doing, and ask if you might be contributing to the problem in some way. Stay calm, listen, and be honest about how you feel. This kind of conversation can be a great start in healing a damaged relationship.

We want you to offer grace and truth to the people in your life, but there are some people who are too sick to receive it. And those people are unsafe for you to be around. If you are being abused by a family member, the first thing to do is find a way to keep yourself safe. Start by telling an adult what is happening. Keep telling people like teachers, school counselors, and youth directors until someone helps you. Doing this isn't betraying your family. It isn't ungrateful or disrespectful. It's the best way to stop the abuse. No one needs to stay in a situation where they are being hurt. If it's happening to you, there is help and hope out there. Just keep talking to trusted adults until you discover the one who will help you.

Chapter 15
Giving Grace

Treat people as if they were what they ought to be and you help them to become what they're capable of being.
— *Johann Wolfgang von Goethe*

As you see your family through your new sense of awareness, it will be natural to focus on all their failings. That's where grace comes in. It doesn't just help you be a little more patient and forgiving—it changes the way you look at people. And when you see your family through grace-filled eyes, you discover you have a lot to be grateful for.

Try a little exercise. Go in your room and sit down. Get out a piece of paper and pen. Now look around your room for things that remind you of something your parents, or grandparents, or other family members have done for you. Then write down what you see and are grateful for. Once you've covered your room, walk through your house. Look in your closet. Check out family pictures. Chances are you'll see reminders of family trips, celebrations, times of connection, signs of your changing relationship. All of this will help you think about the people in your family with a little more compassion and a lot more grace.

Moms
I (Sissy) visited a friend of mine who happens to be the mom of

two girls your age. We hadn't seen each other for a while, so I told her I'd just follow her around while she did whatever she needed to do at home. Eventually we ended up in the laundry room. I sat on the dryer while she spent an hour ironing clothes for her daughters, her husband, and herself.

I left her house feeling totally convicted. My mom must have ironed over a thousand pieces of my clothing while I lived at home and I never once said thank you. Well, maybe I did—in a halfhearted way, like "Oh, thanks Mom" when she hung my clothes on my doorknob. But I never realized how much time she must have spent doing that—and a million other things I probably still don't think about.

What has your mom done for you? It might be something practical such as ironing, driving, cooking, or helping you with homework. It might be something a little deeper like giving you some wonderful books that helped you think, or teaching you to pray, or taking you to church every Sunday. Maybe your mom worked a full-time job and came home every night to do all of these things on top of her workday. Maybe your mom volunteered at your school or led your Girl Scout troop. Whatever she's done—and if she's like most moms, she's done a lot—it's probably made a real, daily difference in your life.

Think about these things. Write them down. And start to show your mom your gratitude. She didn't do it all perfectly, but she did her best. You can express your gratitude in words or in the way you act. Your mom doesn't do any of this so you'll tell her how wonderful she is. But you can sure make a difference in her life when you thank her for the ways she's taken care of you over the years. It's that good old idea of returning thanks.

Dads

My (Melissa's) dad didn't say a lot to me. He didn't encourage

me with his words or tell me every day how much he cared about me. Every once in a while I'd get frustrated about this. So I would go over to my grandmother's house. I would complain about my dad for a while. My grandmother would listen, and then she would say simply, "Lissa, your father loves you. He loves you and he's good to you." And she was right.

My dad wasn't perfect. He did what he could to show me he loved me, but sometimes it didn't feel like enough. He was good to me in his way, although it wasn't always the way I would have liked it to be.

How is your dad good to you? How does he try to show you that he loves you? Because you're a girl and your dad is a boy (how obvious is that?), his expressions of love might be different from yours or your mom's. He might not hug much. He might not say much. But he's got his ways of showing you love.

When your dad asks you if you want to drive to the store with him, that's love (he wants to spend time with you). When he shows you what he's working on in the garage, that's love (he's sharing his interests with you). When he invites you to watch the game with him, that's love (he wants to teach you about the things he enjoys so you can enjoy them together). And when he asks you a million questions about where you're going and who you're going with and who this boy is and what time you'll be home and what kind of car does he drive, that's love too (he worries about you every time you leave the house).

Dads, like boys, just communicate differently. They have their own ways of showing they care and are thinking about you, but they do and are—even when they tell you more with their actions than their words. And you're a lot more likely to see that care when you look at them with grace.

Grandparents

We both remember our parents encouraging us to visit our grandparents when we were your age. I (Sissy) remember going to Hot Springs, Arkansas, to see my mom's mom. After about 30 minutes of talking to my grandmother, I was ready to get back home to my friends. It wasn't that I didn't love my grandmother. I just had so many other things to do.

You might feel the same way about your grandparents. And while spending time with them might not be all that exciting, it is important time that you'll cherish once they're gone. Believe it or not, your grandparents are one of the greatest gifts you will receive in the form of another person. We both have such fond, vivid memories of our grandparents. Now that both of us have lost almost all of our grandparents, we realize we would give just about anything to have them back.

All grandparents are different. Yours might have watched cartoons with you when you were little. Your grandmother might be a fantastic cook. Your grandfather might have played checkers with you or let you sit in his lap when he was driving a tractor on the farm. Even now it might be your grandmother who is teaching you to knit or your grandfather who is teaching you to drive. No matter what they do with you, it is pure joy for them. They delight in you. They love to see you and spend time with you. When you were little, you felt the same way about them. You still do, but it's sometimes just not as convenient.

Enjoy them. Make the effort to go visit them no matter how far away they live. Call them. Email them—if your grandparents are hip enough to have email. Stay in touch. It means more to them than you'll ever know. And it will mean a lot to you as you remember the times you've shared with them.

We know there are also grandparents who aren't safe. If

your grandparents—or anyone else in your life—are abusive, you need to do whatever you can to stay safe. Don't put yourself in any situation where you are harmed. If something happens to you at your grandparents' house that hurts you or makes you feel uncomfortable, tell your parents or another adult you trust. If an adult tells you to keep your experience a secret or that it will make things worse if you tell, tell a safe adult anyway. It will help you and will eventually help the rest of your family, too.

Brothers and sisters

When you were little, you probably fought with your siblings several times a day. But as soon as the fights were over, you would run back outside to play together again. Then at some point in your life together, you couldn't stand each other. This point always seems to occur during long car rides. He gets too far over on your side. She's singing and won't stop. He kicks your seat, she takes your blanket. Siblings just know how to get on your very last nerve.

You're older now. Your siblings might not be, but you are. So your little sister still wanders into your room when you don't want her to. Your younger brother still makes fun of you and embarrasses you in front of your friends. If you have older siblings, they might continue to treat you like the pest they believe you still are. But now that you're older, you can think about your siblings in a new way, even if they present the same old problems.

We spoke with an adult friend of ours recently who said she was horrible to her little sister when they were growing up. This woman is not a mean person. We have never seen her be unkind to anyone, but she says she was mean to her sister. It's not like she locked her sister in the basement for days on end or flushed her goldfish down the toilet. No, she was the pester-y, frustrated, annoy-your-little-sister-because-you-can kind of mean. She told us it took her sister years to get over it.

Your relationship with your brothers and sisters will very possibly be the longest relationship you have in your life. You probably don't know the person you might marry one day, your parents will die, your friends will come and go. But you've either known your siblings since they were born or they've known you since you were born—and one day they will be your last connection to your childhood. In other words, your siblings have a special place in your life. You don't want to damage what can be one of the most fulfilling relationships you'll ever have because someone took your favorite sweater without asking.

Most of us have no idea how much we are affected by our brothers and sisters. Some studies suggest our siblings have more of an influence on who we are and how we develop than just about anyone else in our lives, except our parents. That means you have the chance to be an incredibly positive influence on your siblings. When you give your little sister some attention and show an interest in her life, you're giving her a huge boost in confidence and self-esteem. When you ask your older brother for advice, you show him that you respect his opinion and care about what he thinks.

Brothers and sisters help you learn to be less selfish. They remind you that the world doesn't revolve around you. They can challenge you to be more patient, more kind, more compassionate. If you let them, they can help you become the person God created you to be.

Naturally, you will have conflict with your siblings—that's what happens when people live together. But you have shared a history that will connect you forever. Treat each other well, knowing that you'll both remember these days. Show them grace and love and acceptance. We know you'll get annoyed with each other from time to time. But you can still be grateful for the ways they have influenced who you are becoming.

Extended family

When I (Sissy) was in college, my mom's side of the family consisted of my mom, my grandmother, my little sister, me, and an uncle. My mom's brother was the only one who didn't live with us. He would often be invited to family gatherings, say he was coming, then not show up. One Christmas he had talked to my grandmother several times about how much he was looking forward to seeing her. My mom made a huge Christmas dinner, set a beautiful table for his family and ours, and we waited. We must have waited for a very long time. The turkey got cold. My grandmother got very sad. Then we heard the doorbell ring.

My mom answered the door, but instead of finding my uncle there she saw our dearest family friends, the Longs. Mrs. Long had called my mom an hour before and my mom had told her what happened. Knowing my mom would be disappointed in my uncle's no-show, the Longs left their own family gathering to join ours. They all stood in the doorway in their hats and scarves singing *Jingle Bells* at the top of their lungs. It made our Christmas that year. And it was a perfect picture of how important extended family can be.

Your extended family may be your family's best friends. It may be your aunts, uncles, even teachers you feel close to. It's all the people in your life who walk alongside you as you grow up.

I (Sissy) have a godmother I'm crazy about. Melissa has two aunts in her life who played a huge part in her becoming who she is today. We both had other adults—the parents of our close friends, relatives, coaches, youth leaders—who we could talk to and trust. Think about all the adults you have in your life who truly care about you and want the best for you. When you feel like you can't talk to your parents about something, you can turn to your extended family for help.

So talk to them, ask them questions, learn from them—be grateful for the family that extends far beyond the walls of your house.

No thanks

I (Sissy) counsel a girl whose family doesn't really get this whole idea of gratitude. It's not a part of who they are or how they act—toward each other or anyone else. They do what they want without thinking about other people. I recently met with this girl's mom, who told me she had decided to only do those things that made her happy. In other words, she's putting her needs first.

Imagine what your life would be like if your parents had been like this mother and had decided to only think of themselves, to only do what was convenient for them or made them happy. If you were sick in the middle of the night, there would have been no one there to comfort you. Who wants to wake up at two in the morning to help someone else fall back to sleep? When your best friend hurt your feelings, your mom probably wouldn't have wanted to hear about it, especially if she was watching her favorite TV show at the time.

But most parents don't act that way. They wake up to help you even when they're exhausted. They listen to your heartache even when they are hoping for a moment to themselves. They drive you around town when they have other places they'd rather be. They do all of that because they love you. And that's the kind of love God calls us to. It's helping when you don't feel like it, listening when you'd rather not, giving when it's inconvenient.

The reason that gratitude requires effort is that it's not about us. It's about others. It's about looking at someone else and expressing your heart and gratitude for them. Since you are coming out of those self-conscious, narcissistic years, it can be even more of an effort for you. Your brain has been pulling you in the opposite direction. But you're starting to notice the ways other people care for you. And you can give grace. You can have gratitude for all of the ways people give to you, even—and sometimes especially—your parents.

You're at the age when you are starting to understand more about who God has called you to be and the way he has called you to treat people. But, again, you do have a choice. You can live your life to be happy and do the things you want, or you can live your life in a way that shows gratitude and love to others. We hope you will be that kind of person because we believe that's who God created you to be. And when you live your life with grace and gratitude, you'll find you have plenty to be grateful for.

The effects of gratitude

Gratefulness spreads. Maybe you noticed this when you did that exercise of writing down things you were grateful for. You spotted a stuffed animal your dad gave you when you were little and that reminded you of the time you spent together at the fair. Once you start thinking of the ways people have cared for you and the things in your life you're grateful for, you realize the list is actually pretty long. And that's when gratitude truly takes over.

That's because gratitude is more of an attitude than an action. Once you begin to say thank you, thankfulness becomes a part of who you are. Gratitude awakens something inside you that is infectious. And then you no longer have to work at being grateful—you just are. Other people will pick up on your gratitude because your attitude—and actions—reflect it.

So think about the specifics of your family. What are you grateful for? What do you notice? Gratefulness might not come naturally, yet. But the more you practice it, the more natural it will become. And it won't just make a difference to your family, it will make a tremendous difference to and in you, as well. Consider these words from Jesus. They sum up what it means to grow into a person who thinks of—and is thankful toward—others.

You're familiar with the old written law, "Love your friend," and its unwritten companion, "Hate your enemy." I'm challenging that. I'm telling you to love your enemies. Let them bring out the best in you, not the worst. When someone gives you a hard time, respond with the energies of prayer, for then you are working out of your true selves, your God-created selves. This is what God does. He gives his best—the sun to warm and the rain to nourish—to every-one, regardless: the good and bad, the nice and nasty. If all you do is love the lovable, do you expect a bonus? Anybody can do that... In a word, what I'm saying is, Grow up. You're kingdom subjects. Now live like it. Live out your God-created identity Live gener-ously and graciously toward others, the way God lives toward you. (Matthew 5:43-48, *The Message*)

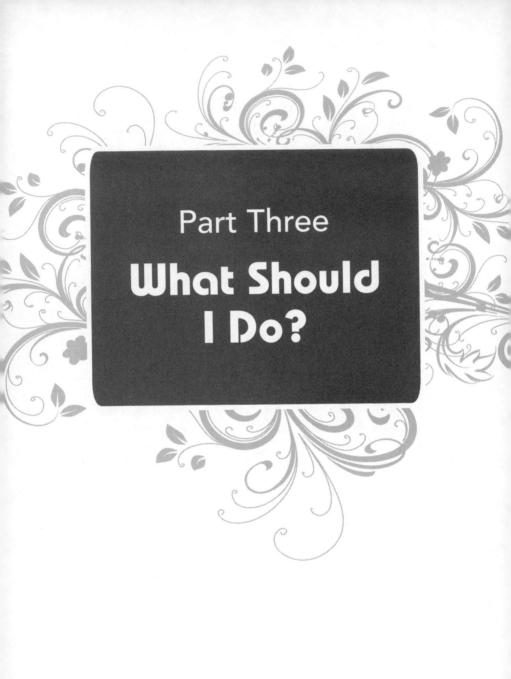

Part Three

What Should I Do?

Chapter 16
Harmless Habits

I believe that the greatest trick of the devil is not to get us into some sort of evil but rather have us wasting time...If he can sink a man's mind into habit, he will prevent his heart from engaging God. — Donald Miller, Blue Like Jazz

How do you waste time? Is it on your cell phone? Reading magazines? On Facebook or MySpace? Or are you doing something else, like drinking or cutting? Maybe the better question is not how do you waste your time, but *why* do you waste your time?

There's an interesting story in the Gospel of John. (Actually, there are a lot of interesting stories, but we'll go with this one for now.) Remember the story of Mary and the racing disciples finding the empty tomb? A few days after Jesus' resurrection, he disappeared again. Now the disciples had already had their world flipped around when Jesus rose from the dead. So when he left them a second time, they had no idea if they'd ever see him again. Can you imagine how they must have felt? Confused. Sad. Frustrated. Alone. Lost.

So what did these disciples do with all of that? Did they get out their Bibles to search for answers? Did they gather to worship and pray together?

Nope, they went fishing. In John 21, Simon Peter turned to his two friends and said, "I'm going fishing." Their response? "We'll go with you."

How many times have you been in a similar situation (okay, not similar circumstances, but having similar feelings)? You're confused, you feel alone, sad, frustrated. So you say, "I'm going ...." You can fill in the blank. Or, maybe you don't say anything. You just sit in front of your computer. You go back to something you know or do something that helps you feel safe. You sink into a habit. That habit can be constructive—although cell phones and computers aren't always very constructive— or destructive.

When you were in seventh and eighth grades, you may have felt some pressure to do or get involved in the kind of things we're talking about: The media, communication, athletics and academics, drugs and alcohol, hurting yourself, and eating disorders. But by now, these things are potentially more than just pressure: They're habits.

When life is going our way—when we feel close to God and other people, when we feel good about ourselves—we don't depend on those habits quite so much. But then life stops going our way, we get our feelings hurt, something happens at school or at home—and back we go to our habits.

We want to talk specifically about each of these habits. We're going to look at the action (or habits themselves), the reasons you might be involved in this habit, and the results of getting hooked (pardon the fishing pun), and we'll help you discover another way to meet whatever need that habit seems to fill in you.

Take fishing for example. The actual act of casting the nets was the action. In the case of Peter and friends, the reason they went fishing wasn't really to catch fish as much as it was to retreat into something familiar, to get their minds off the pain and confusion they were feeling. The result was that these men spiraled down into their own discouragement.

Then Jesus came along (yes, he did come back) and showed his friends another way.

Our hope is that we can help you identify the habits you go back to when things get hard. We want to help you find a way out of those habits and into a place where your heart is able to engage with God.

There are two different kinds of habits we find girls picking up. The first kind is the habit you already know you shouldn't be involved in—drinking, drugs, hurting yourself, that kind of stuff. We'll talk about those habits in the next chapter. But the other kind of habits can be a lot sneakier. These habits are the ones that seem harmless—and can be if they are used thoughtfully and carefully. They are habits that are part of your life already, habits you might be so caught up in you haven't even noticed how they have started to affect you.

Media

The action

Do you subscribe to *Seventeen* magazine? What about *People* or *Us Weekly*? Do you get lost for hours on your favorite celebrity gossip Web sites? We know one high school freshman who is only allowed on Quizilla one hour per week. It may sound strict, but before her parents made this rule, she was spending at least five to six hours a day logged on to Quizilla's quizzes and blogs. She was losing her identity in the identities of the women and girls featured on the site.

The reasons

Our Quizilla friend doesn't like her life. She only has one friend at school. Boys pick on her pretty ruthlessly. She told us, "Other people's lives are much more interesting than mine. I'd rather think about theirs." Quizilla provides her an escape. She doesn't

have to wonder about her lack of friends or why the boys treat her the way they do. She can escape into blogs about high school girls whose lives seem to be working.

Quizilla might not be your habit. It might be some other form of online connection with friends—real or virtual. It might be that you watch television every chance you get when you're home. Maybe you read books like *Gossip Girl* so you can experience the lives of teenagers who seem a lot more exciting than anyone you know. Maybe you love to read magazines about the lives of celebrities, hoping a little of their glamour might rub off on you.

We all need a little entertainment here and there. The problem is when they are no longer a fun distraction but a necessity. You can't get online and you panic. If you go somewhere without your book or magazines you obsess over what you're missing.

You need enjoyable outlets. But you don't need to lose your life in someone else's—even if you believe that life is more exciting than your own. Your real life will suffer and become a whole lot less exciting if it gets swallowed up by these habits.

The results

An addiction is basically anything that we need more and more of to make us feel okay. We typically think of addictions involving chemicals like drugs and alcohol. But a person can be addicted to almost anything. Whenever you need more and more of something to feel okay, you become less and less of yourself. That thing takes over.

If magazines, Web sites, and books such as *Gossip Girl* were the only voices telling you who you should be, what would they say? Two things would be important: The way you look and the way you act. The way you look would be a pre-puberty body. You would be all legs, no body fat, and definitely no curves. Depending on the current trends, you would have to have long, straight hair today and maybe short, curly hair tomorrow. Whatever the magazines and Internet decided was perfection on any given day would be the standard for everyone. There would be no variety in sizes, shapes, clothing styles, or even haircuts.

As far as the way you would act, the word we use is *flippant*. Nothing would really bother you. You would make choices with boys, drugs, and alcohol that would not only upset your parents but would be terribly destructive. You would have a semi-smile plastered on your face at all times. It wouldn't be a real smile because that would suggest genuine emotion. It would be a mysterious, elusive kind of smile. If media is your habit, you know the look we're talking about.

Basically, you would look and act superior to everyone else. There would be no warmth, no compassion, no creativity, and definitely no individuality. The world—and you—would be boring.

Immersing yourself in the media can make you feel like its version of beauty and style and perfection is the standard to live up to. And that only leaves you feeling bad about yourself. No one can master that kind of body—or that kind of aloof emotion. That's not how anyone—girl or guy— was meant to live.

Another way

1) Don't let the media dictate your image. Be yourself. God made you to be different from everyone else who has ever been or will ever be. Be that person. Discover who you are because you'll feel best about yourself when you're acting like you, rather than like

some computer-perfected, media-driven version of yourself.

2) Find other role models. Talk to older girls and women who are interesting, smart, and creative—and who don't buy into the media ideal (we'll introduce you to a few of them in the next chapter). Watch movies and read books with characters who think for themselves, like *Pride and Prejudice* and *Little Women*.

Technology

The action

Okay, be honest. Are you addicted to your cell phone? Do you count the minutes until you can check your MySpace or Facebook? Do you carry your iPod everywhere you go? If you're anything like a lot of the girls we know, the answer is a solid "Yes." Girls who would normally never break rules at our camp sneak in calls on their cell phones. (We don't want them to use their phones while they're at camp. We want their focus to be on camp, not home.) Their phones are like baby blankets for these girls—they feel totally lost without them. What about you? When you're having a hard day, do you try to call or Facebook someone—anyone—just so you don't feel lonely?

Again, cell phones are fine. The Internet is okay, too—as long as you're being careful. And I (Sissy) usually pull out my iPod when I'm on a plane so I can avoid talking to people I'll never see again. But all of these can become problems if you're using them to escape, to keep yourself from having to think or to feel or connect.

You might think they do just the opposite—that you think and feel more when you are constantly communicating with your friends or listening to your favorite music. And you probably do—in both cases. But you need time when you're not connected to other people—when you're alone with your thoughts, your ideas, and God.

The reasons

You want to connect. You want to have instant access to your friends. You want to know the status of people in your network. You want to know what they're saying on their blogs and what's written on their walls. You want to be able to text, blog, IM, call, and communicate whenever and however you can. You are wired for relationship, and the technology of today makes relationships even more accessible—and sometimes more dangerous.

And sometimes you don't want anyone to bother you. You want to sink into yourself and not have to deal with the stress that comes with relationships. So you pop in your ear buds and check out.

The results

What isolates you from awkward situations also isolates you from potentially good situations. When you're hooked up to your MP3 player, you might miss a great conversation or the chance to make a new friend. You might not notice that a guy you think is cute is trying to get your attention. You might miss something really funny your dad says or something really kind your grandmother says. You will miss the life that's happening around you.

The Internet, too, can create all kinds of problems. You've probably heard the stories—the 19-year-old guy your friend thought she knew from chatting turns out to be a 45-year-old man with a daughter her age (this really happened to a girl we know). There are a million stories out there about the risks of the Internet. And maybe you're smart or savvy enough not to meet with a person you only know through Facebook. But that doesn't mean you're not at risk for the other dangers technology brings into your life.

Another concern we have about technology is that it can cause girls to lose sight of who they are and how they normally relate to people. Think about what you say to people online. You probably say things you wouldn't think of saying in person because you feel bolder sitting behind a computer in your own house than you would looking that person in the eye.

We counsel several really sweet girls with good morals who have said very sexual things to guys through the Internet. They would never say these things to a guy's face. They didn't even mean what they said—they were trying to be funny and flirty. But one of these girls had the guy she'd been flirting with show up at her door, thinking she wanted to do all the things she'd talked about doing. She was terrified.

There are other, more subtle changes as well. With text messages, for example, you bypass the "Hi" and "How are you" that are part of thoughtful communication. You cut right to the point: *Mt you at Stbucks at 10. Thx.* Right? Maybe you don't even go to the trouble of typing the *thx*. Over time, this kind of communication changes the way you relate. You begin to lose patience when people take their time getting to the point of a conversation. You start talking faster and wishing other people would do the same. You get so used to short-hand communication that you have little interest in long, drawn-out conversations—the kind that help us form deep relationships.

Another way
Technology isn't going away. In ten years it's going to be even faster, easier, more accessible, and less personal than it is now. And for all the ways it makes our lives easier and more fun, it

will continue to create new challenges for how we relate to other people. Use it wisely. Be a girl and a woman who is known for her graciousness. Treat others with respect. Treat yourself that way—in person and on the Internet. Don't be one person in real life and another in virtual life.

Give yourself space and time to think. Silence your phone and sing or pray in the car. Take a walk without your phone or your music and listen to the kids playing in their yards and the wind in the trees. Spend time reading and writing in your journal without having to answer the phone or the bings of your computer. Think. Breathe. Discover. Feel. And then go back to relating.

Because you crave relationships, cell phones and the Internet are always going to be some of the main ways you connect with people. If you take time to discover who you are, you will have more to offer your friends on the other end of the conversation.

School culture: Athletics and academics

The action

Where do you put the most pressure on yourself? Is it grades? What about basketball or cross country? The school play? The dance team? Cheerleading? It's easy for adults to forget the immense pressure teenagers feel on any given school day. Whether it's in athletics, academics, or some type of arts, you want to excel. This leads to stress, to pressure, and to a habit that can quickly move from a wonderful part of your life to one that takes over.

The reasons

Last year a girl named Brooke came in for counseling because she was having panic attacks. They typically happened toward the

end of school each day. After talking to her it was pretty obvious why she was having these attacks. Brooke was vice president of her class. She kept an A/B average. She played lacrosse and soccer for school, and she had just tried out for the spring musical. When she came to see us, several of her coaches and advisors were fighting over Brooke's time. The soccer coach thought she should be playing on the travel team. The drama teacher needed her at rehearsals. Her parents wanted her to study. Brooke had no idea what to do. She felt like any decision she made would let someone down.

Because relationships are important to us, we want to please the people we care about. We want our parents to be proud, our teachers to know we're trying, our coaches to believe we're doing our best, and God to be honored in our decisions.

It sounds like a really good thing and it definitely can be. It's good to be conscientious and do your best and care about the important people in your life. But trying to please everyone all the time—and the pressure that brings with it—can easily become a distracting and addictive habit. It can make you feel like you're more important than you really are and that you've got to live up to every bit of that role.

This habit is sometimes the result of a little leftover narcissism and sometimes the belief you won't be loved if you don't perform in just the right way. The truth is your coach might be disappointed if you don't go out for the traveling team, but she'll move past that disappointment very quickly. Your parents might be unhappy if you bomb a test, but they'll still love you. And you're probably not the only person in school who can perform the role in the play or take pictures for the yearbook. The pressure to be all things to all people comes on strong when you believe you—and only you—can make them happy. Of course, that isn't true. Other people can step in and do things. And you can still have good relationships without always being the one who answers the need.

The rush that comes from feeling busy, feeling needed, feeling indispensible can be a little addictive. And that's what the real habit is here: The pressure. Some girls thrive on pressure. They need that pushing and shoving of all their commitments because it feels kind of good to have all that attention and activity.

In reality, it might start off feeling good. But that changes quickly. What felt like a response to your gifts feels like a requirement. That's real pressure—the kind that creates stress, anxiety, and sometimes even panic attacks. And that's why we think this is a habit worth breaking.

The results

If you've been living like this, you already know what the results are. Stress. Trouble sleeping. Falling grades. You flub your lines. You miss a goal. You forget a commitment. Maybe you can't eat. Maybe you eat too much. You're short with your friends and shorter with your family. With so many balls in the air, it's only a matter of time before some of them start to drop.

Another way

Doing your best in school, being a good friend, honoring your family, following God—these are all hopefully included in the list of priorities for your life right now. But no one expects you to do all of them perfectly. You can be a good student, a good friend, a good daughter, a good artist, a good whatever it is that you do without being perfect. We know that because, while we know thousands of good students and friends and daughters, we have yet to meet one who is perfect. Expecting perfection from yourself only creates the pressure that takes the joy out of the very activities you're trying to enjoy.

So give yourself some of that grace we talked about in the last chapter. You will disappoint your teachers and coaches and even your parents from time to time. You will mess up. Everyone does. But you can still honor God and your parents and be who God created you to be even when you make mistakes. In fact, you're more of that person when you let go of the perfectionism and pressure. God wants your engaged heart, not your perfect report card or flawless performance—and certainly not your habitual stress.

The problem with eating disorders is at the root. Just because the branches aren't there, doesn't mean the root is not growing.
— Rebecca, age 17

Drugs. Alcohol. Cutting. Eating disorders. You probably don't need much of an introduction to these habits. You've been warned about them for years and know all the reasons you shouldn't be involved with any of them. Just the same, you might have friends who drink or you've been drunk yourself. You might think about cutting yourself or you've decided to stop eating so you can lose weight. Even if you haven't been involved in any of these habits we want you to know what brings them on. Like our friend Rebecca said, the roots of these habits can grow long before the branches show up

Drugs and alcohol

The action

We have yet to meet a girl who drinks or uses drugs who doesn't know—somewhere inside of her—that she shouldn't. Every teenager knows it's illegal to drink and do drugs. But that doesn't seem to stop those who decide to give it a try. It doesn't stop those who justify their behavior with excuses like "Everyone else does," or "Pot's not addictive," or "What I'm doing is nothing compared to the rest of the kids in my school."

All the warnings about the dangers of drugs and drinking seem to make very little difference when you're a teenager. Yes, these substances really do mess with your brain and your body (even pot) and they can lead you to make terrible—even tragic—mistakes. Still, you are at an age where it seems like none of those bad things will ever happen to you or your friends. So all that logic doesn't necessarily help you stay away from the very real temptation to take a sip of beer or try your first joint.

Maybe this one will. Alcohol and every drug from marijuana to meth have the same effect. They provide a temporary escape from life. They numb the pain. Actually they numb everything—the pain, the joy, and the good judgment that comes with a clear head. There is no faster way to miss out on and mess up your life than to develop a destructive addiction.

Right now drugs and alcohol can seem like the quickest way to have fun, to live out the image of what teenage life is "supposed" to be—parties, guys, friends. They seem like the fastest way to stop feeling hurt or alone or left out or nervous around other people. But they aren't any of those things. They are quick fixes that end up making just about everything in your life a whole lot worse.

The reasons

There are a lot of reasons why girls and guys drink or use drugs in high school. One reason is they believe everyone else is doing it and they're afraid they'll look unpopular, or uncool, or unsomething if they don't. These people use mostly on weekends with groups of other people who are using—the people they are trying to impress.

Then there are those who use as a response to something

or someone. Maybe they're angry at their parents. Maybe they just want to be seen as "edgy." These people use—even if no one else is—because they want to get a reaction from someone. They're doing it for the shock value and the cool factor they think drugs and alcohol provide.

The third kind of person who uses does it to escape. She can be at a party or alone in her room. It doesn't matter. She just wants to stop whatever pain she's feeling—and she'll do just about anything to make it happen.

Whatever the reasons for using, the results are the same. Drugs and alcohol are destructive—not only for the user but for everyone who cares about that person, too.

The results

Have you ever seen a snowball rolling down the hill? It gets bigger and bigger and faster and faster the farther it goes. Drinking and using drugs does the same thing. You go to a party. Your friends try their first beer. You think "why not?" and try one, too. When you get home your mom asks you about the party and you immediately tell her you went to the movies instead.

You might be reading this section and thinking you don't have an addiction. You've only been drunk a few times. But your habit has already started to snowball. Drinking one beer turns into drinking more beer or harder liquor. Using pot leads to more pot or more serious drugs. And the lies have to get bigger and bigger. It becomes a miserable lifestyle which means you need even more drugs and more alcohol to make it feel less miserable.

Then, like that snowball slamming into a tree at the bottom of a hill, you get caught or hurt or make a terrible mistake and life—or at least life as you knew it—falls apart. Your parents find out you've been drinking and lying and you lose their trust. You cheat on your boyfriend without really knowing what you're doing. You black out. You get into a car you think is a taxi and end up sexually assaulted by a stranger on the side of the interstate. These are real consequences. We know the girls living through them and living with the pain brought on by mistakes they made under the influence of drugs and alcohol. We know you don't think any of this will happen to you. None of these girls did, either.

Even if you think you're getting away with it, you will still suffer consequences. The pain you're trying to avoid by using still exists the next morning. And even if your parents don't catch you, you wake up with the guilt of knowing how disappointed they would be if they knew. You have the pressure of constantly coming up with stories or excuses to cover it up. And you're learning to depend on something outside of yourself to get you through hard times. All of this combines to make you feel a whole lot worse about yourself than you did when you tried to escape in the first place.

Another way

If all of your friends drink or use drugs, find just one new friend who doesn't. We promise you there is at least one other person at your school who doesn't want to do these things. And it is so much easier to say no when you've got someone who will say no with you. Believe it or not your friends will end up respecting your decision in the end—and respecting you for doing what you believe is right.

If you want to live on the edge, go rock climbing. Ask your parents if you can get a piercing. Dress funky. Do something, anything that doesn't put you in a state where you lose control of your ability to make decisions. There are plenty of ways to be edgy without risking your parents' trust or your life.

And if you want to escape, there are ways to do it that don't make your problems worse. A little exercise goes a long way. It actually increases the chemicals in your brain that make you feel good. As dorky as it sounds, it really does create a natural high. Not up for that? Then call a friend. Paint a picture. Watch a silly movie.

Of course, we also believe you can never truly escape your pain. The best way to deal with it will always be to deal with it. Talk to someone—your parents, a school counselor, a teacher, a youth leader. Tell someone what's going on in your life and let that person help you find healthy ways to work through it. That's the only way pain ever gets better.

Drugs and alcohol do provide a temporary escape. But the damage they cause—the guilt you feel and the consequences you face—aren't worth it. And they only make you want to escape that much more. It's a terrible—and terribly addictive—way to live.

Hurting yourself

The action

"I'd rather see myself hurt physically than feel myself hurt emotionally." That's what we hear when we counsel girls who are hurting themselves. They cut. They scratch. Some of them even bite. These are all forms of what is referred to as self-mutilation.

It is a phenomenon among teenage girls today. You probably know someone who is referred to as a "cutter." You've at least heard about them. It can sound edgy, even glamorous, in a "tragically misunderstood" sort of way. It's not.

The reasons

The girls we know who have struggled with self-mutilation do so for one or more of these three reasons: They want control, they're angry with themselves, or they want attention.

Even if you haven't hurt yourself, you might relate to some of these feelings. Your life might seem out of control. Maybe your parents have gotten divorced recently. Maybe you've been abused or made fun of at school. These are the kinds of problems girls who hurt themselves tell us about. They feel as if their emotional pain is out of their control, so they try to control their physical pain. It's a little bit like pinching yourself so you won't feel your toothache. (If you've done this, you know what we're talking about).

You might be angry with yourself. You might feel like you've let down the people you care about most. Maybe you've made some pretty bad mistakes. Maybe you don't feel like you can live up to your own expectations. It's so much easier to get mad at yourself than to get mad at other people—even when they're the ones who have hurt you.

Maybe you relate more to the third category of girls who hurt themselves. You feel desperate for attention. You haven't had the kind of friendships you see in other girls. Your mom travels all the time or your dad died when you were younger. You just don't feel loved or even liked by anyone. If you do something to hurt yourself maybe people will pay attention. Maybe they'll notice and give you the love and encouragement you want so badly. And maybe they'll feel a little bad, too, for having ignored you for so long.

The results

If you relate to any of what we've said in this section, read the following carefully. Cutting or self-mutilation of any kind is a serious, addictive problem with tragic results. The most obvious result of hurting yourself is that you actually do get hurt. The cuts leave scars—and they last much longer than the situation that brought them about. Those scars can be really embarrassing later.

And once again, the habit you believe will stop the emotional pain only puts it off. The sadness or anger or shame or whatever you're feeling just goes deeper inside and takes even longer to work through. And you will have to work through it, otherwise it will continue to come out in random ways; you will blow up at your mom over something little or fall apart when a friend cancels your plans on Friday night.

Spiritually, hurting yourself takes you to dark places. It feels good in a deceptive, angry, almost evil sort of way. It is secretive and takes you down a path that has nothing to do with God. God wants you to be moving toward the light. He wants you to experience healing and hope. Self-mutilation takes you in the opposite direction. Darkness always becomes darker the farther you go into it. Hurting yourself works the same way. The more you do it, the harder it will be to stop.

Another way

God gave you feelings for a reason—they connect you with other people and they connect you with God. They are a part of what motivates you to grow and mature and work through the challenges that life brings.

One summer at camp we talked about the oil warning light you have in your car. You need that light to know when you are low on oil. Without it, your car would eventually break down. Your feelings—anger, sorrow, even joy—are a lot like the oil light on the car. They point you toward something deeper, something that requires your attention. Don't ignore

them. It would be like taking a hammer and shattering the oil light.

When you find yourself struggling, talk to your parents or a friend. If you don't have a friend you can talk to, ask your parents to take you to a counselor. If you don't want to talk to your parents, talk to another adult you trust. There are people who care about you and want to help. Paint. Journal. Write poetry or songs. Feelings always feel worse when you keep them inside, and those feelings can bring about more creativity in your writing and art.

If you feel like you don't get enough attention, do something constructive that gets you involved with other people. Take up a sport. Volunteer with younger kids. Develop your own sense of style. Do something to express who you are and let people see what you have to offer. It's normal to want to be noticed and appreciated. But you also have to feel good about yourself. Do what makes you genuinely happy and you'll find you don't crave the attention of others quite so much.

We all want control of our lives. We all want attention. We all get angry with ourselves from time to time because we all make mistakes. And we can let those feelings take over. But we don't have to. We can face those feelings and deal with them in ways that help us grow.

The truth is that you're a mess. We're messes, too. And that's why there's grace—to cover the messy parts of who we are. You don't have to hurt yourself to pay for it—Jesus already did.

Eating disorders

The action

You know the action on this one as well as we do. Maybe you

sit at a lunch table where one of the girls eats only apples—if anything—for lunch. Maybe you have a friend who sneaks off to the bathroom after every meal to throw up. Maybe it's you doing these things. Maybe you have thoughts like "I wish I were anorexic. At least then I would be thinner." Or you worry because you think about food more than most people.

Girls naturally think about food a lot. We like it. It's comforting. It's even fun, in a relational kind of way. Food gives us an excuse to connect with our friends. When's the last time you hung out where there was no food involved? We like eating out, baking cookies, and hanging out in the kitchen. But some girls can't just enjoy food. They are controlled by it. And these are the girls who fall somewhere along the eating disorder continuum.

We typically think of eating disorders as bulimia—eating a lot and then throwing it up—or anorexia—not eating much of anything. But there are a lot of other types of eating issues, too. Eating disorders can also include overexercising, regular binging (eating too much on a constant basis without throwing up), and bouncing back and forth between trying not to eat and trying to purge your body of everything you've eaten. There is also something called "eating disordered thinking," which is an intense preoccupation with food

The reasons

Girls end up struggling with food for all sorts of reasons. One girl with bulimia told us she and food "just don't get along." She was having a hard time adjusting to the changes in her body. She blamed food for the way her little girl's body was developing adolescent curves. Another girl we know struggled with anorexia for several months because a friend repeatedly told her she was fat—even though she was only a size four.

The obvious causes for eating disorders are as simple as an insensitive comment or as serious as sexual abuse. But underneath those causes are deeper problems—and they have nothing to do with food. Girls who have eating issues are much like the girls who hurt themselves. They want control and they are angry at themselves.

Girls with eating disorders push themselves to do well—academically, athletically, and relationally. They are often perfectionists. They try to keep up the image on the outside, but inside they are struggling desperately. And they are furious with themselves for struggling. In their minds they fail too much, they want too much from others, they are too easily disappointed. We can see that their expectations of themselves are not only unrealistic but are also unachievable. But they can't see it. They want perfection.

These girls also want control, and the only thing they feel they can control is food. The trick is that food ends up controlling them. They restrict what they eat but continually obsess about the food they do eat. They spend a lot of their day trying to figure out the next opportunity to go somewhere and throw up. What begins as an attempt to look better results in an all-consuming, exhausting entrapment of control and self-hatred.

The results
Like so many of these habits, the biggest result of eating disorders is how much of your life is absorbed by it. One 15-year-old told us:

I realized today that I've been wasting a lot of my life trying to achieve this goal of being thin. I've spent so much time and energy focusing on it and it now controls my life. It controls all my

thoughts. I'm stuck and I can't get out. Every time I think I'm doing good and I have the strength to get through, I fall back down
again. I'm sick and tired of living this way. I wish I could just accept
the way I am and not freak out so much about my weight. I have so
much regret for how I've been living my life. I'm giving myself over
to this god of thinness.

Your body will probably never look like a supermodel's—
remember their bodies don't look like that, either. You won't
ever look like anyone but you. You can diet and exercise all
you want, but that won't make your legs longer or your hip
bones narrower. You will always have places that are rounded
and soft, and they won't necessarily be the same places that
are rounded and soft on your best friend. It's a part of how
God designed you as a woman.

But it's easy to forget how God designed you when you're
battling the omnipresent supermodel image and your own
need for control. So you keep trying to lose weight to achieve
the look you want—and you can't get there. You try harder.
You eat less and less or throw up more and more. You focus
on your weight until it's all you can see. You give yourself over
to the "god of thinness." And that god requires everything.
Once you develop an eating disorder, every thought, every
decision, every emotion relates to food. It is a prison that feels
like it will trap you forever.

Another way

If you are focusing more and more on your weight, here are
some ways to avoid the prison of an eating disorder.

1) Don't turn food into an emotional outlet. If you're sad,
don't eat a bag of chips. Talk to your friends. Talk to your
parents. Draw. Write in your journal. If you're angry at your-

self, let those feelings out, too. It's easier to get angrier with yourself than with someone who has genuinely hurt you. But you need to work through things in relationships, not just cover them up. If you're angry at someone, skipping meals or throwing up isn't going to change anything—but talking to that person might. You may need to change in some ways for your relationships to be better, and there could also be ways others need to change. In reality, there's probably a little of both. But none of that will happen if you use food to deal with your problems. Let your feelings out in healthy, productive ways. You'll discover more about yourself and about God.

2) Exercise. Moderate exercise—30 to 60 minutes a day, five days a week—not only helps your body stay in shape, but it also helps your emotions. When you exercise, endorphins are released into your brain. Those chemicals make you feel better about yourself.

Exercise is also a great stress reliever. When you're upset about something, take a walk outside. It can clear your head, it gives you time to look at the problem a bit more objectively, and it helps you think about how you want to handle the situation.

At the same time, it's easy for a food disorder to turn into an exercise disorder. There's no reason for you to work out for hours at a time and no reason for you to hurt your body in an effort to stay in shape. Stick to that 30-to-60-minute mark and you'll be healthier and happier.

3) If you want to lose weight, talk to your parents. Too many diets—especially those that involve skipping meals—deprive you of the nutrients that keep your brain and body functioning normally. And that makes you tired, irritable, and unhappy. So ask your parents to take you to your doctor or a nutritionist—someone who can help you develop a diet and

exercise plan that will work for your body

4) Stop comparing yourself to other girls. It never helps. It's like comparing apples to oranges, *American Idol* to *24*. It just doesn't work. Girls and women come in all shapes and sizes. The idea that only one shape, one size is acceptable is a lie you don't have to buy into. Focus on being healthy instead. You'll feel better about yourself and the way you look.

5) Remind yourself that what you look like is only a small part of who you are. You may have had people—even people who love you—tell you you're overweight. And maybe you are heavier than is healthy. But that doesn't mean you aren't beautiful. Your beauty has much more to do with your heart and personality than it does your weight. Your happiness has more to do with how you feel about yourself than the size of your jeans. It has to do with who you are and how you treat people and what you do that makes a difference in the lives of others.

If you've read this section and think you might have an issue with food, talk to someone. Make an appointment with your school counselor. Talk to your parents or your youth director. Find an adult you trust who can help. Recovering from an eating disorder—even keeping yourself from developing one—is hard work. You can't do it alone. You need friends to walk alongside you and adults who understand this all-consuming struggle. With their help, you can get to a place where you feel confident with who you are—whether you weigh 90 pounds or 190.

We've talked to so many girls who struggle with food. It's an awful battle. Please don't start it on purpose.

The best way

We started this conversation talking about Jesus' fishing friends.

Let's pick up that story where we left it. Peter was sad and confused. Things weren't working out as he had hoped. So he and his friends went fishing. They decided to waste their time—and distract themselves—with something easy and familiar.

We hope as you've read the past two chapters you've discovered what kind of "fishing" you've been doing. We all do something. We all have habits we turn to when life isn't working the way we think it should. But now is the time for you to recognize what your habits are and start working on ways to let go of them—or at least lessen your dependence on them. Because, just as Peter and his friends found out, those distractions never bring the fulfillment we're looking for:

> So they went out and got into the boat, but that night they caught nothing. Early in the morning, Jesus stood on the shore, but the disciples did not realize that it was Jesus.
> He called out to them, "Friends, haven't you any fish?"
> "No," they answered.
> He said, "Throw your net on the right side of the boat and you will find some." When they did, they were unable to haul the net in because of the large number of fish. (John 21:3-6)

Not long ago I (Melissa) met with a young woman. She was 25 and going through her second divorce. She was dealing with a huge burden of shame and regret. But the real source of her shame went back to her teenage years.

"In high school I basically did whatever I wanted," she told me. "I drank. I smoked cigarettes. I smoked pot. I slept with my boyfriends and messed around with other people's boyfriends. I stole from my friends. When I look back on my life, all I can see is how badly I hurt other people. Back then I lived like it didn't matter."

She was fishing. She was doing anything she could to feel happy, fulfilled, or just distracted so she didn't have to feel. But it didn't work. Years later, her choices have continued to make her pain worse. And now, at last, she is changing her approach. She's talking about the hurt in her life, working through the struggles so she doesn't need to fish anymore.

You might feel a lot like the disciples out on the lake. The night has been long. You're not catching anything. Your ways of fishing—losing yourself in school or the computer or alcohol or what you eat—aren't working. The morning comes and you haven't got any fish.

But Jesus is standing on the shore. He is calling to you and showing you another way—the best way. The way to fulfillment is not to lose yourself in wasted time or destructive habits. The way to fulfillment is found in trusting Jesus. He calls out to you and tells you to cast your net—love other people, be the person you know you were created to be, be brave enough to face your problems, take your eyes off yourself and look at the goodness around you. That's when the fish come.

Chapter 18
Words of Wisdom

He was thinking about almost anything, except himself, and that was one of the best things that had happened to him in two long years. — Gene Stratton-Porter, The Keeper of the Bees

We asked a friend of ours in high school who she turns to for advice. Her answer might surprise you. "Several years ago I trusted my friends the most. I asked their advice on everything and really believed they knew a lot more—or at least they knew me a lot better—than the adults around me. I don't feel that way anymore. I love my friends and trust them. But they really don't know any more than I do. I would rather get advice from someone who is close enough to my age to understand me, but has already been through what I'm going through now."

We'd guess you're starting to feel the same way. So we've asked some older people (not that much older—they're all in their 20s and 30s) what they know now that they wish they had known in high school. These are interesting, creative, unique women of great beauty and strength who we wish you could meet. They have lived out a lot of the words and stories in this book, and we thought they would have some great and entertaining truths to share with you.

"I wish I had based decisions on the question, 'Will I regret this later?' There is much more to life than high school.

In other words, don't let high school be the be all, end all, because it's not."—Juliana, 38, elementary school teacher

"I wish I'd known that if I changed my mind it didn't mean I was a failure or had been wrong in the first place. Now I 'know' (in the sense that I forget the lesson slightly less often than I used to) that adapting my take on something isn't a sign of being fickle or unresolved, but rather a willingness to admit I'll never have the final word on anything."—Gretchen, 25, editorial assistant

"I wish I had known that others weren't thinking about me as much as I thought they were. I wish I had known that I mattered. And I wish I had known that it makes a difference when I tell people how much they mean to me."—Jessica, 20, college student

"If I knew then what I know now, I would have spent a lot more time not thinking about boys and more time investing in who God created me to be—my interests, my goals, my purpose."—Tami, 36, actress, mom

"I wish I knew that in the grand scheme of things, time goes so fast and that a summer spent doing something adventurous could be life-changing. Those couple of months away from school friends would have been worth it."—Jackie, 39, mom

"I wish I had known that who you are in high school does not dictate who you will be later in life, that we have so many chances to rediscover and reinvent ourselves. I wish I had known that the moments that mortify us will be forgotten by most people. That what is devastating at 16 can make you laugh at 25. I wish I had known that your body can and will change. What you look like at 16 or even 18 does not dictate what you will look like later. I wish I had known that God really does care about the details and anticipates our needs better than we do. And I wish I had known that whether or not you were asked to the prom just won't matter later in life."—Lauren, 25, high school English teacher

"I wish I knew that the boy I was dating wasn't really going to be my husband even though we sure acted like it all the time. I was way too committed to boys at that stage in my life. I wish I would have enjoyed the girls in my life more."—Pace, 29, development director

"When I was in high school I wish I would have known that all those things that seemed so important back then really do fade away. Also that life gets better as you go. Each year I learn more and enjoy more than I did the year before—even during the really rough times."—Audra, 37, community and development director of music venue/ skate park/ coffeehouse/ hangout

"I wish I had known how to say no, and when I didn't say no to not feel like God was disappointed in me for being human. I wish I had known that it was okay to win. I was always too aware of the fact that if I won, someone else would have to lose. I wish I had known how to save money, and how to say what I felt instead of holding it in."—Cindy, 38, singer, songwriter, mom

"I wished I had learned how to ask for help. Now I struggle to ask for help because I never learned how in high school.

I reach an impasse in relationships because there is a certain genuiness, honesty, and authenticity that is brought to relationships when you can ask for help."—Julia, 25, counselor

"In high school I wish I had known that my life as an adult would be really great even though it has ended up looking a lot different than I thought it would. I spent a lot of time back then worrying about finding a boyfriend and then a husband. I'm still not married but I have the best life. I wish I had really been able to rest in the fact that God was in control of my life and that he had good plans for me that I could trust."—Mary Katharine, 35, childhood ministry director

"Gossiping is a way of getting someone's complete and utter attention for just a few minutes. But when someone invests a secret in you and you keep it, the trust that is being built is something that will last, build integrity, and deepen your relationship. It's not worth the five minutes of fame to be the first to spill the beans."—Clare, 25, associate program manager

"I wish I had known in high school that life is not going to be like high school. Things that seemed so important then seem so insignificant now. Not making cheerleader, not getting asked to a dance—those things were disappointing then but looking back, I see they helped me to grow and become the person I am today."—Ashley, 37, loan review officer, mom

"I wish I had known that graduating, getting out of the cliques and annoyances of high school, and making a fresh start in college was not the final answer. College *has* been absolutely wonderful. I've made much stronger friends and feel like I am more comfortable being myself. But I still struggle with my self-image as well as with a whole new set of problems that come with this phase of life. I wish I had known that I will never be able to 'fix' myself and that I can't keep looking toward the next big phase of life to end my current problems. I wish I had built a better foundation of being satisfied where I am and trusting the Lord to be my hope."—Aubrey, 21, college student

"I wish I would have known that I could say no to whoever I wanted to, whenever I wanted to."—Tracey, 37, missionary, former model, mom

"I had so much self-hatred and sadness because my parents were divorcing. In my head I knew that what I was going through was not my fault, but I wish I had known it with my heart. I wish as a teenager I had been able to show more grace to myself in the midst of self-hatred. I wish I had enjoyed learning and not tried so hard to make perfect grades."—June, 32, artist

"I wish I had known that friends with whom you can truly be yourself are invaluable. Being loved as you are and loving others for who they are and not what they can do for you or how they make you look is what creates lasting friendships. There is such freedom and rest in knowing you can be yourself with a friend. That freedom comes by offering your true self to a trustworthy person and letting them be who they are without shame or embarrassment. Another thing I wish I had known in high school was that it's okay to not get things right. I was so obsessed with appearances and my performance in school, sports, and social settings. It gets exhausting and is impossible to keep up that image."—Betsie, 24, assistant junior high youth director

"I wish I had taken more chances in getting to know other people. I stuck to what was safe: People I knew and who knew me. I wish I had more confidence in my ability to reach out to others."—Elizabeth, 23, grad student

"I wish I would have known that people would still love me even if I didn't perform well or look just right."—Briana, 25, school counselor

One thing we both wish we knew in high school was how to learn more from the wisdom of others. We hope you will learn something from these women. Their words are filled with truth. Grace is important. God is important. Popularity isn't. You don't have to earn anyone's love or approval, especially God's. You are loved and delighted in more than you'll ever know. You are free to be you.

Part Four

Who Do I Want to Be?

He stood appalled, judging himself with the thoroughness of God, while the action of mercy covered his pride like a flame and consumed it. He had never thought himself a great sinner before but he saw now that his true depravity had been hidden from him lest it cause him to despair…He saw that no sin was too monstrous for him to claim as his own, and since God loved in proportion as He forgave, he felt ready at that instant to enter into Paradise.
— *Flannery O'Connor,* The Complete Stories

I learned I was a sinner this summer. I didn't learn it because I lost my virginity or tried pot for the first time. I learned it because I made my mom cry. Actually, my sister and I did. We got in a huge fight and my mom, who never cries, started crying. She said our arguments were tearing our family—tearing her—apart and that she couldn't take it anymore. I was shocked.

I had spent the last year of my life pretty angry. It wasn't really about anything specific. I had been hurt by several friends in a row, didn't get along very well with my sisters, and had been ditched by a guy I liked. I tried to be okay at school, to look like I was happy—or at least not miserable. I guess I saved it all up for home. My parents told me I had a bad attitude but I just kept going. I didn't really know what else to do.

But then my mom cried. Several weeks later, my dad and I were talking and he told me how much it hurt him to watch me be so angry. And then my little sister talked about how it hurt her to watch a friend of hers struggle with an eating disorder. I had one of those, too.

Those few months were honestly the first time I ever realized how badly I hurt people. I grew up in the church. All my life I had heard I was a sinner. Jesus died on the cross for my sins. I knew it, but I never really *knew* it.

Things are different now. I really want a good relationship with my sister. I don't want to hurt my family or anyone else I care about. I know I can—and do. But what I know the most now is just how badly I need a Savior.—Sarah, 17

When you're not doing any of the top four trust-violating behaviors—drinking, smoking, drugs, and sex—it's easy to think you're a pretty good kid. And to some degree, you are. You're making hard choices when a lot of people around you are taking the easy way—or habit—out.

The purpose of this chapter, though, is to tell you that you're not as good a kid as you might think. And even more important, it's to tell you why that is really great news.

A great sinner

I (Sissy) went to a camp in Texas called Camp Waldemar. It was an amazing place—huge, cypress trees lining a green river, majestic, stone buildings that had been standing for decades. I loved it—and still miss it every summer.

I was not, however, the Ideal Waldemar Girl. There is one every year. The Ideal Waldemar Girl is voted on by all of the counselors from camp each summer and is elected because she fits the high ideals and values represented by the camp. She rides down the river in a white canoe, in white clothes, while all of the other campers sing a song that says something like "To the sweetest girl in all Camp Waldemar." I know—it sounds a little over the top, but it really is a high honor.

My hometown was outraged that I missed this honor. At

least, I heard trickles of outrage from folks from my home-town. They thought I should get it. The people who knew me thought I fit that description of the Ideal Girl. I knew I didn't. Or at least I had serious doubts.

I mean, I was a nice enough camper. I didn't put Nair in anyone's shampoo—though one girl in my cabin did just that. I didn't smuggle alcohol into camp in sunscreen bottles like some of the older girls. But I knew myself. I got jealous. I felt insecure and competitive. I talked behind other people's backs. I could be mean to my parents and angry with my friends. I knew all of this but I still spent a lot of time trying to live up to the "ideal."

I felt like two people—the one I presented to the world and the one I knew I was inside. I had a hard time distinguish-ing which one was really me. What I didn't know then is that they both were.

In high school I believed that real sinners were the people I would have called "wild." I thought I was just a sinner in the spiritual sense, which meant I wasn't really that bad. That belief came—in part—through the encouragement of all the sweet folks who thought I should have been the Ideal Walde-mar Girl. But the more I bounced between feeling better than other people and feeling like a bit of a fraud, the more I felt like there must be something wrong with me.

There was. I was a real sinner, too. You see, God doesn't categorize sin the way we do. Sin is anything we do that pulls us away from the life God wants for us. So my jealousy was just as bad as someone else's cocaine use. Romans 3:23 says, "For all have sinned and fall short of the glory of God." That *all* includes me. I fell—and still fall—just as short as the wild girls.

I (Melissa) had a different understanding of sin growing

up. I had been hurt—deeply hurt—by someone I loved. I spent many years of my life trying to understand and undo the damage caused by that relationship. I was trying to find healing so I went to my friend Dan.

Dan's response was completely different from what I expected. After listening to me with tenderness and compassion, Dan said something I will never forget. He said, "Melissa, I want you to remember what you're feeling. You're capable of doing the very same thing that was done to you—and you're capable of doing much worse."

That was hard for me to hear. But I knew Dan was right. All have sinned—the person who hurt me, the person hurting someone else in that way, and me. Something inside told me I had the same potential to hurt others. And that was not what I wanted. That was when I really began to understand what Jesus did when he died to put an end to sin. I thought the answer to my healing was to talk until I felt better. Instead, the answer to my healing—and yours—is the cross.

Finding hope

This might be hard to believe, but your greatest joy and your greatest hope in life will come from seeing the depths of your sin. Deep down we all know we're sinners, that we're a mess. That's the good news. And what comes next is the action of mercy.

When Dan said I was capable of great sin, I felt more hope than I had in months. Because I knew I could make choices. When I only saw myself as a victim, there was no hope. I was destined to live a life of hurt and pain. But with hope I could move through the pain and learn to treat others—and myself—differently. As long as Sissy kept trying to live up to some ideal (knowing inside she couldn't do it), there was no hope. But when she knew she could make a choice, she felt like Jesus was standing with her, saying, "Turn around. Believe me. Follow me. You're going to be hurt. But you have a choice to live differently."

Christians so often look like we have it all together. But the reason we're Christians is because we don't. At some point we realized we needed Jesus. Sometimes we fall back into thinking we have to put on a good front, that there's shame in admitting our failures. But the shame is in not admitting them. Because until we know how messed up we are, we can't really hand our lives over to God. As long as we keep believing we can be perfect, that we can have it all together, we will keep believing we don't really need Jesus.

Jesus carried on the cross with him everything you have done and everything you will do that keeps you from experiencing the kind of life God wants for you. He cried out, "My God, my God, why have you forsaken me?" (Matthew 27:46) as he felt the full weight of all the ways we have forsaken God. When Jesus died, our sins—our anger and jealousy and mistakes (even those "big four")—were nailed onto the cross with him. They no longer have to separate us from God. And that is the action of mercy that covers us and makes us free.

The following words are from the journal of Sarah, whose courageous, honest words you read at the beginning of the chapter. She was studying Ephesians and came face to face with her own sin—and God's mercy:

When Paul is writing to the people in Ephesus, he keeps pointing them back to their old way of life and how they lived when they were unredeemed people. He talks about how dead in their sins they were and how they sought after worldly things but that God, with his amazing love and mercy, made us alive again and saved us by his grace. The awesome part about it was that even though

Paul was writing to the people of Ephesus hundreds of years ago, he might as well have been writing it to each of us individually, because I think that it is as much our story as it was the story of the people who lived hundreds of years ago. We can look back on our lives and see where he forgave sins that we couldn't even forgive ourselves of and how he redeemed us, even when we thought there was no hope of redemption. It's so amazing when you stop and think about it. It makes me so thankful when I look back at the person I used to be. It truly is by Christ alone that I am no longer the same person I once was.

Throwing fruit

We talk about this good news at every one of our camps. But last summer we talked about it with a bowl of fruit sitting in front of us.

The Bible talks about fruit a lot—good fruit and bad fruit. The good fruit are the fruit of the Spirit you might have read about in the book of Galatians—love, joy, peace, patience, kindness, and so on (see Galatians 5:22). The bad fruit are those things we feel shame about. The things we have done or others have done to us. They are sin.

Jesus takes that sin to the cross. The problem is that we sometimes hang onto them.

We want to forgive others but we get stuck in the hurt, where it's easier to be angry than it is to forgive. We want to be forgiven, but we feel stuck in our shame, where it's easier to be angry with ourselves than to walk in forgiveness. The writer Anne Lamott says, "Forgiveness is when it finally becomes unimportant to hit back." She doesn't just mean hitting someone else, she means hitting ourselves as well. And as we've said a lot in this book, we girls are pretty good at hitting ourselves.

You know you are a sinner. You know Jesus died for your sins and the sins that have been committed against you. But how do you let them go? That's where the fruit comes in.

Last summer each of the campers had an opportunity to think and pray about their sin. Then they each came up to the front of the room and chose a piece of fruit. They took their fruit, walked out on the deck overlooking the lake, and tossed their fruit as hard as they could into the water.

As we threw fruit, we basically were doing ourselves what God does for us. Micah 7:18-19 says, "Who is a God like you, who pardons sin and forgives the transgression of the remnant of his inheritance? You do not stay angry forever but delight to show mercy. You will again have compassion on us; you will tread our sins underfoot and hurl all our iniquities into the depths of the sea." We were tossing our sins into the depths of the sea—or lake. We can't even tell you how great those splashes sounded from the deck as our "sins" hit the water. They were gone. And so are yours. Jesus, in his great mercy, wipes the slate of your great sin clean. You are forgiven. You are free.

You may need to toss a little fruit of your own to remind yourself of that (you can blame us when your mom asks where all her fruit has gone). Or you can write your sins down on a piece of paper and then rip it up. The point is to remember that you are forgiven—completely. You are no longer the same person you once were. You will mess up again. But the action of God's mercy and the depth of God's love wipes away all the mess, the shame, and the sin forever.

Chapter 20
You Matter

You are the only you this world will ever know. And something
about your life is meant to make something about God known
in a way that no one else can.
— *Dan Allender,* How Children Raise Parents

Someone I (Melissa) love attempted suicide last year. It was devastating to me and to everyone who cares about her. She is right around your age, and she stopped believing she mattered. When people give up on life, it means they no longer think their life makes a difference, that no one will really miss them when they're gone. This was not and still is not true of my friend. And it's not true for you either.

But we all have moments when we wonder.

A good self-image?

Last summer, on the drive up to camp, we talked to a group of girls your age about what they would like to learn about during the week. Some wanted to talk about relationships with others, some wanted to talk about their relationship with Christ. But there was one thing every girl mentioned: Self-image.

Many parents bring their children to Daystar for the same reason. "She has a bad self-image. If you could just help her…"

What we want to say is, "Yes, we can help. When she is

in her peer group or at camp, she will be loved. There will be people who will accept and encourage her and help her know she makes a difference."

But, it's never enough, is it? We could tell each girl who comes through Daystar how much she matters or how much she makes a difference. We could tell you on every page of this book. You might believe it for a little while. You'd close the book and feel pretty confident as you walk downstairs and get in your car. You might even feel that way as you walk into the gym for the basketball game. But then you see the guy you like. You see other girls who give you weird looks. And all your confidence goes out the window.

Remember my (Melissa's) friend Dan who told me what a sinner I was? Well I had dinner with him several years later. I told him I was trying to work on my self-image. So he started saying really nice things to me—things I won't bore you with now. But he ended by telling me he wanted me to say out loud that I was beautiful. You can imagine how I felt—probably a lot like you would. I got *really* embarrassed. I refused at first. Then he got louder. "If you don't say those words, Melissa, I'm going to shout them to the whole restaurant." And he would have. So I said it. I said out loud that I was beautiful and actually went home feeling a little better about myself. My self-image had gone from a 4 to somewhere around a 6 on a scale from 1 to 10. But as I looked in the mirror that night, I still saw the same me looking back.

All of us struggle with self-image. We all feel bad about ourselves some days. We don't look good. We don't have as many friends or dates as other girls. We aren't as smart as we wish we were. Our lives don't look as together as we think they should. We're not sure anyone would miss us if we weren't here. We all have those times when we simply stop believing that we matter. We think if someone could tell us how beautiful or kind or funny or valued we are all of that would go away. If we just felt loved enough.

But that never happens. We might feel loved enough temporarily, but then we get our feelings hurt. Time goes by and we forget. Or the love simply wasn't enough to take away all of our insecurity.

Jesus takes a different approach when it comes to our self-image. Over and over in the Bible he says two words: "Follow me." He stands on the shore and says it to his fishing disciples. He says it to the tax collectors and sinners. He says it to you, and he says it to us.

Jesus could say, "Hey, all of you in the boat who are beautiful, follow me." Or, "Those of you who have good personalities, I choose you. You'll be easy for me to use." But he doesn't. He doesn't choose us because of how we act or the way we look. He loves us because he sees who we really are beneath all the things we think create a good self-image.

It's hard to believe Jesus would choose us. It's hard for us to believe our lives can make a difference, that if we follow Christ our lives will have an impact on other people. So we do the best thing we can think of. We wait. We wait till we are stronger, or more open, or more spiritual, or whatever we believe will make us more usable by God. But he still says, "Follow me."

The only you

The quote at the beginning of this chapter has become something we talk about a lot with girls your age. You are the only you. No matter what's going on in your family, no matter how the other kids at school treat you, no matter how you look or act or even feel, God can and will use you in a unique and glorious way. The only path to knowing you matter is allowing yourself to matter.

Susan came to Daystar because she was struggling with the death of her father. She was seriously depressed and wondering if she really mattered, if her life was even worth living. She got involved in our groups during the school year and signed up for camp that summer. She made a huge impact at her camp. She was kind and insightful and helped make the other kids feel comfortable just by being herself. So we asked her to help with one of the camps for the younger kids later in the summer. She did. She came back to the ninth-and-tenth-grade camps, too. That week she met another girl struggling with a death in her family and experienced for the first time what it felt like to be used by God.

"This was the most amazing week of my life! I finally feel like my life and my past make sense. Thank you for letting me be here so I could see that I can make a difference."

Susan never imagined God could use her—the good and hard parts of who she is and what she's been through. But he did. All she did was answer when he said, "Follow me." She showed up at camp and God used her. And that made her feel better about herself than anything we could have said to her to convince her she mattered. She had to see it for herself.

That's the secret. It's the secret to how we help people in our counseling and it's the secret to a better self-image. You matter. You can matter. God can use you—just like you are now—to make a difference to someone else.

Melissa's teaching at that camp wasn't really about self-image, even though it was what the girls wanted to talk about. It was about the fact that our images will never live up to what we believe they should be. But we follow anyway. We love. And give. And serve the people God has put in our lives. As we do, we start to see that our lives have impact. We start to see that we can and do make a difference. And in the end, that is what leads us to feeling better about ourselves.

One night at camp I (Melissa) had each of the kids at camp say out loud, "I matter." They were uncomfortable and embarrassed, just like I was at dinner with Dan. And then, as the week went on, they experienced the words they had said. They had opportunities to make a difference to each other and see that they mattered.

Don't worry so much about how you feel about yourself. None of us really feels that great anyway. Don't worry about how much people love you. You will feel good as you learn to love and give to other people. Find places you can do that. Volunteer with younger kids. Help out at your church. For that matter, help your parents around the house. Look around your school for people who need a friend, around your town for places that need a hand. Then just give of yourself, because you can and do make a difference. You matter.

Jesus does not—anywhere in the Bible—say he wants us to have a good self-image. What he says is, "Follow me." Our lives matter when we fall in line behind Jesus, trusting he can use every part of us—the good and the hard—in a way that will make something about him known, in a way no one else can.

*What's lost is nothing to what's found, and all the death that
ever was, set next to life, would scarcely fill a cup.*
Frederick Buechner, Godric

Molasses is a sheepdog. She's supposed to herd sheep. But Molasses has no sheep. She only has kids—the kids at our summer camp. So she herds them.

If one of the kids swims too far out in the water, Molasses swims out and brings her back. If one jumps into the lake screaming, Molasses thinks she's drowning, so she jumps in the water after—and usually on top of—the person she's planning to save. If you've never seen a sheepdog, think the Shaggy Dog—only bigger. We actually have lessons on the first day of camp on what to do if Molasses tries to save you, because she could actually drown you if you're not expecting her.

Several years ago, I (Melissa) had some friends who are like family to me staying at my hosue. They were there with their three young children, and we were all asleep in various rooms. All of a sudden Molasses went crazy. She ran over to me barking as loud as she could—over and over again. I tried to get her to be quiet, but couldn't. She jumped up on my bed and stood on top of me barking (it was a little like being saved by her). When I could finally breathe again, I said, "Okay Molasses, what is it?"

She ran to the door so I followed. When I looked out the door into the hallway, I saw little bitty two-year-old Brittney, sitting outside my room at the top of the stairs, all by herself in the dark. She could have easily fallen down the entire flight. I picked her up and put her back in her bed. I tried to get Molasses to come back to my room but she wouldn't. She lay down across the doorway of Brittney's room, making sure she wouldn't get out and get lost again. Brittney was safe. Molasses was happy. Brittney was lost—and found by Molasses.

We're all a little like two-year-old Brittney sometimes. We get lost. We lose our way. We lose ourselves. But Jesus relentlessly comes to find us.

> Then Jesus told them this parable: "Suppose one of you has a hundred sheep and loses one of them. Doesn't he leave the ninety-nine in the open country and go after the lost sheep until he finds it? And when he finds it, he joyfully puts it on his shoulders and goes home. Then he calls his friends and neighbors together and says, 'Rejoice with me; I have found my lost sheep.'" (Luke 15:3-6)

We thought about calling this book something else. It shouldn't be *Growing Up Without Getting Lost* because you will get lost. Between the hiccups in confidence and high points of development, mean girls and media, boys and body image, you will have days when you lose who you are. You might get lost for months or even years.

But you will never be lost to Jesus. He knows when you start to wander away from the person you were created to be. When you yell at your mom for something she didn't do, he knows that's not who you are. When you feel like no one cares about you or loves you, he knows the truth. When you experiment with drugs for the first time, Jesus knows he created you for so much more.

So he sets out. He leaves the other sheep to come looking for you. And he can find you—no matter how far away you've gone.

Jesus wants to be your shepherd. He wants to find you and help you find yourself. He wants you to feel confidence, hope, joy, sorrow, passion, life. And he will use all of these to show you who you were made to be.

Listen. Look to him. Look for him. He will speak to you softly as you see all he's created around you. He will speak loudly through the people who love you. He will use those people, that creation, his Word, and the Holy Spirit stirring in you to speak truth about who you are and what your life can be about. But you've got to listen. You've got to look.

You are the only you this world will ever know. You are beautiful. You are created for relationship. You are talented. You are unique. Something about you will teach the world something about God in a way that no one else can. We could really call this book, *Growing Up and Being Found*. You are found. You do matter. And all of that is true even when you feel lost.

Notes

Chapter 1
L. Frank Baum, *The Wizard of Oz* (New York/London: North-South Books, 1996), 13.

Chapter 3
Elizabeth Goudge, *The Heart of the Family* (New York: New York, 1953), 1.

Chapter 4
Elizabeth Berg, *Durable Goods* (New York: Avon, 1993), 4.

Chapter 5
Henri Nouwen, *Intimacy* (San Francisco: HarperSanFrancisco, 1969), 13.

Madeleine L'Engle, *A Circle of Quiet* (New York: HarperCollins, 1972), 33.

Michael Gurian, *The Wonder of Girls: Understanding the Hidden Nature of Our Daughters* (New York: Pocket Books, 2002), 78-79.

Chapter 6
Mary Pipher, *Reviving Ophelia* (New York: Ballantine, 1994), 254.

Chapter 7
Hannah Hurnard, *Hinds' Feet on High Places* (Wheaton, IL: Tyndale House, 1975), 112.

Chapter 8
Frederick Buechner, *The Sacred Journey: A Memoir of Early Days* (San Francisco: HarperCollins Publishers, 1991), 72.

Chapter 9
JRR Tolkien, *The Return of The King* (New York: Ballentine Books, 1994), 160.

Chapter 10
Antoine de Saint-Exupery, *The Little Prince* (San Diego/New York/London: Harcourt, Brace and Co., 1971), 87.

Chapter 11
Sharon Hersh, *Bravehearts* (Colorado Springs: Waterbrook, 2000), 17.

Chapter 12
Elizabeth Goudge, *Island Magic* (New York, Grosset and Dunlap, 1955), 352.

Lemony Snicket, *A Series of Unfortunate Events: The Austere Academy* (New York: HarperCollins, 2000), 52.

Chapter 13
Jane Austen, *Pride and Prejudice* (London: Penguin Books, 1985), 258.

Chapter 14
Henri Nouwen, *The Return of the Prodigal Son* (New York: Image Books by Special Arrangement with Doubleday, 1994), 85-86.

Chapter 16
Donald Miller, *Blue Like Jazz* (Nashville: Thomas Nelson Publishers, 2003), 13.

Chapter 18
Gene Stratton-Porter, *The Keeper of the Bees* (Bloomington: Indiana University Press, 1991), 100.

Chapter 19
Flannery O'Connor, *The Complete Stories* (New York: The Noonday Press, 1993), 269-270.

Anne Lamott, *Plan B* (New York: Riverhead Books, 2005), 47.

Chapter 20
Dan Allender, *How Children Raise Parents* (Colorado Springs, CO: Waterbrook Press, 1999), 189.

Epilogue
Frederick Buechner, *Godric* (San Francisco: HarperCollins 1980), 96.

Suddenly, it seems like everything in your life is changing. Your friends expect way too much from you. You fight with your parents more than you'd like. You just don't understand why your life seems so chaotic now. You are not alone. If you're feeling overwhelmed or confused with your life, this book will help you understand who you are, and give you hope for who you're becoming.

Mirrors and Maps
A Girl's Guide to Becoming a Teen
Melissa Trevathan & Sissy Goff
RETAIL $16.99
ISBN 978-0-310-27918-1